Here's to fewer assumptions!

REVIEWS

"It may sound like an unusual compliment for a business book, but this is a beautiful, insightful piece of work. I typically speed through the "stories" in business books to get to the meat of the point. But in this book the stories grabbed my attention and didn't let go. Ellen bravely and powerfully shares lessons she learned the hard way. Then she tops it off with solid advice for improving your communication skills and ultimately, business *and* personal relationships. Be ready with your highlighter and pen to make this a well-worn resource."

—Mary Kutheis, Business Owner + Executive Coach

"Everyone needs to read this book! After reading it, I realized how I constantly 'assume' things about people and situations, and often incorrectly, in my daily life. Whether it be business or personal, I have learned many valuable and practical ideas and suggestions about how to step back and take the time to see the other person's perspective. The Introduction of the book hit me square in the face 'Unmet expectations are almost always the result of assumptions.'"

—Karen McBride, Business Owner

"In 2022 a book about assumptions acts as a lighthouse to a better perspective on other people and their intentions. Ellen's vulnerability and insight as the lighthouse keeper guides the reader to a better place. This book is a must read for anyone who works, plays, communicates, or lives with other people ... which is you, you need to read this book."

—Eric Hultgren, Director of Brand Strategy +
Social Media

"In these extraordinary times, we need truth tellers, people who can hold their actions up to the microscope and analyze the moving parts, identify the disease and help eradicate it. In the field of coaching Ellen has been both student and teacher. The lessons she imports from her years working as a community organizer and honing her craft as a coach, and in her everyday life, give her readers relatable examples while giving us the tools and courage to embrace ourselves, right or wrong, learn from it, and use it to make our world a better place."

–Rebecca Gale-Gonzalez, Humanist + Environmentalist

"This book did not disappoint. It was informative and entertaining. Ellen has a great ability to relate and it is demonstrated in the way she shares her stories. I feel I will benefit in both my business and personal life with this information. She reminds us of the basics we need to follow and teaches us how to turn a negative into a positive to keep us moving forward. Great read!"

–Suzanne Shew, Business Owner

"I wish I had read Ellen's book *I Thought You Knew* years ago! Coming from Corporate America, I made A LOT of assumptions of my interactions with colleagues. Ellen was spot on when she encouraged the reader to slow down and reflect more. We need to ask more questions. Her stories were so interesting and insightful. I absolutely loved the questions she had sprinkled throughout chapters. I plan to incorporate some of these awesome questions in my coaching business. Thank you, Ellen, for a great book!"

–Julianne Phillips, Business Owner + Executive Coach

"Ellen weaves honesty and humor with proven strategies to improve professional and personal relationships and grow your leadership capabilities. Practical advice for immediate impact and long-term results. I recommend this to anyone looking to host relevant and meaningful meetings and expand communication channels."

–Nancy Boxey, Executive Director

"Ellen has a knack for bringing out the highest level of self-awareness in people. In her book, she's done this through raw story-telling that encourages the reader to reflect on their own perceptions and influences. Through the book, Ellen shares tangible lessons she learned from authentic experiences and demonstrates that emotional intelligence is gained through simply botching up some-times. Through her writing, she has generously shared a collection of these discoveries and, when read with intent and an open mind, the reader gains valuable lessons to apply to their professional and personal lives."

–Gina Rens, Director of Administration

"I have known Ellen Patnaude since 2017, when she offered to assist with the library's bond campaign. Her skill, per-sonality and attitude were invaluable, and she kept me and the committee in line. Gently and directly.

This book reads the way Ellen speaks, presenting sophisticated concepts in an accessible style and lan-guage. Her honesty and vulnerability give the reader the counsel, encouragement and hope that ridding oneself of one's assumptions creates better relationships at home and in the workplace."

–Melissa Malcolm, Library Director (retired)

"Ellen Patnaude has written a thoroughly entertaining, easy to read, and yet compelling book about assumptions and communication.

Perhaps the greatest strength of the book is her candor in admitting her own mistakes and how she has learned from them. The stories she tells are raw, poignant, and relayed with a healthy dosage of self-deprecating humor. It's a quick, fun read that will leave the reader with much to think about, both in the professional and personal spheres. There's an epiphany on nearly every page."

–Chris McNeany, Leadership Development Facilitator

"I have worked from fortune 500 companies to some of the most outstanding tech startups in my career in sales and marketing. I can attest that assumptions are often the kiss of death for a company or a salesperson. In a world where we now strive to categorize and label everything, the assumptions based on these labels have made every-day interactions much more complicated. This book is an example of the pitfalls of assumptions and how to work through them. If you or your team or company are strug-gling to communicate and understand, start by making this book required reading. The chapters are engaging and poignant, covering assumptions in various forms. Do assume that if you are open to the ideas in this book, you will learn a lot and perhaps assume nothing."

–Tom LaVoie, Regional Vice President Sales

"If you want to relate to people more authentically–more truthfully, well then Ellen Patnaude has done the dirty work for us! By processing and laying bare her own life experiences through the filter of assumptions, she has shown us the way toward our own enlightenment around how we sabotage our relationships–at work and personally–with unconscious assumptions. Through her candid, authentic, and honest reflections, she gives us practical tools to identify our own misguided behavior and shares strategies to right our wrong thinking. She calls our "bullshit" out with both care and respect, and she isn't shy about revealing both moving and humorous personal stories from her broad life experiences. This book is beautifully written, intelligent, and frankly, quite generous."

–Jennifer Sprague, Author #1 Best Seller on Amazon +
Business Owner

"A raw and revealing look into how we can unknowingly sabotage our journey through life, both personal and professional. Ellen identifies those bad habits, and the hard wiring, that leads to us getting in our own way. This is an insightful and amazing book that will change your path in life (when it comes to communication) for the better.

A must read for anyone looking to improve the effectiveness of communication with others to achieve great results!"

—Paige King, Engineering Manager

"What a great, thoughtful read. Through the various vignettes, what assumptions are and how they impact everything from why a meeting is held to why a colleague is labeled as 'not a team player,' become not only clearer but something to really consider after putting the book down. I find myself rethinking past interactions with my family, friends, and coworkers and what part my assumptions played in the outcome. It has the right mix of stories, questions, and connections to really get you invested in the material."

—Alison Kenyon, Administrative Professional

I
Thought
You
Knew...

I Thought You Knew...

CONFESSIONS OF A CHRONIC ASSUMER

*(and How You Can Stop Guessing Your Way
Through Important Interactions)*

Ellen Patnaude

PYP
Academy
Press

For permission requests, write to the below address:

PYP Academy Press
141 Weston Street, #155
Hartford, CT 06141

The opinions expressed by the Author are not necessarily those held by PYP Academy Press.

Ordering Information: Quantity sales and special discounts are available on quantity purchases by corporations, associations, and others. For details, contact the author at Ellen@LeadQuine.com.

Edited by: Noël King and Nancy Graham-Tillman
Cover design by: Nelly Murariu
Typeset by: Medlar Publishing Solutions Pvt Ltd., India

Printed in the United States of America.
ISBN: 978-1-955985-77-2 (paperback)
ISBN: 978-1-955985-78-9 (eBook)

Library of Congress Control Number: 2022913311

First edition, October 2022.

The information contained within this book is strictly for informational purposes. The material may include information, products, or services by third parties. As such, the Author and Publisher do not assume responsibility or liability for any third-party material or opinions. The publisher is not responsible for websites (or their content) that are not owned by the publisher. Readers are advised to do their own due diligence when it comes to making decisions.

Publish Your Purpose is a hybrid publisher of non-fiction books. Our authors are thought leaders, experts in their fields, and visionaries paving the way to social change—from food security to anti-racism. We give underrepresented voices power and a stage to share their stories, speak their truth, and impact their communities. Do you have a book idea you would like us to consider publishing? Please visit PublishYourPurpose.com for more information.

DEDICATED...

To the leaders I've had the pleasure of meeting
along my path, who have helped me realize
I have something to say.

To my community organizing colleagues,
who taught me the basis of everything I know about
how to do this work, and who agitated the shit out of me
to force me to grow, even when I didn't want to.

To my family (born and chosen), friends, and especially
my children, who love me despite my chronic assuming
and are always there to clear things up, mostly gently.

To my dad and in memory of my mom, who have both
always loved me in the best ways they have known
how through everything. Like, everything.

To my beloved Dani, who is my rock, my missing puzzle
piece, my unwavering cheerleader, and my soulmate.
You give me some of your courage when I'm having
trouble finding my own.

CONTENTS

INTRODUCTION

I read an article recently about how unmet expectations can be a silent killer in all types of relationships. This particular article focused mostly on marriage but mentioned the broader implications for all types of relationships. It got me thinking about work relationships and how unmet expectations can affect them.

Because unmet expectations are almost always the result of assumptions.

Let's not start out a book about assumptions by assuming we've all got the same definition in mind. An assumption is defined by Oxford Dictionary as "a belief or feeling that something is true or that something will happen, although there is no proof."[1]

That last bit, "although there is no proof," is particularly dangerous.

Assumptions happen all the time, in every type of relationship. They can happen when we're afraid. They can happen when we're feeling low in confidence and when we're feeling overly confident. They can happen because it's Tuesday. Which is just to say they can happen for seemingly no reason at all.

Regardless of the reason (or lack thereof), many of us make assumptions about the expectations of another person. Very often, this is done without any intention of harm or malice. We simply don't take the time or make the effort to clarify. Instead, we guess, quietly to ourselves, which is an assumption. Sometimes we guess correctly, and sometimes we don't.

For many of us, this behavior is so pervasive we don't even recognize it in our daily lives. At least, not until we stop and think about it. Then it becomes clear. Painfully, blindingly, embarrassingly clear.

What causes us to make assumptions in the first place? You may have your own ideas and experiences with this. I'm going to share mine throughout this book. Hopefully they will spark you to recognize even more places where you, too, might be assuming. Discovering how often I have made

---

[1] Oxford Learner's Dictionary, s.v. "assumption," accessed June 4, 2022, https://www.oxfordlearnersdictionaries.com/us/definition/american_english/assumption.

assumptions (and continue to make them when I'm not careful) has been a threshold experience for me—now that I've become aware of my own tendencies, I can't go back to being unaware of them. It's both a blessing and a curse.

Some assumptions are quite benign and often acceptable. When a client doesn't show up on time, I assume something has happened to make them late. My assumption is present in my communication to them: "I'm assuming something came up today that prevented you from making it to our session on time, and not that you're lying in a ditch somewhere, as my mother used to say. Please reach out when you have a moment to let me know that you're okay, and to reschedule."

We assume people will ask for what they need. If a prospect needs additional information when I've shared a proposal with them, I assume they will let me know. When my bonus daughter wants to come spend the weekend at our house, I assume she will let us know. When my wife needs me to pick something up from the store, I assume she will let me know.

But sometimes it's not safe to assume someone will let you know what's happened. If I've offended or upset a friend, I assume they will let me know. But sometimes they just avoid me instead. If I don't hear from a close friend for a few weeks, I assume she's just busy with life and that if anything were wrong, she would let me know. But sometimes she's not reaching out because she's cracking under the pressures of life and doesn't want to bother me.

In case you don't know me (yet), I'm a coach. I ask a lot of questions. This book is full of them. But I'm not a researcher. Despite my early beginnings working in the field of biology, that interest didn't stick. All I've done is get a lot of this stuff wrong over the past 30 years that I've been adulting. I suppose that's a form of field research. But if you're looking for the hard science behind why we do these things, this isn't the book to shed light from that perspective.

That said, I've noticed trends in common situations that occur naturally for many of us. They happen multiple times in any given day, and every day. I see them, I experience them, and I discuss them with clients who face them. And I'm still screwing up, giving myself a never-ending supply of examples on what not to do.

Frankly, I find stories about messing up way more interesting than stories about getting things right. The Japanese proverb "Fall down seven times, stand up eight" is hanging on my office wall. These are words I live by.

This book contains many stories, as well as a bit of guidance. It's a far cry from the typical "how-to" book. Each chapter includes a few examples of things going wrong (sometimes terribly wrong). Occasionally there are examples of things starting out wrong but ending up right. Every chapter concludes with one example of a way someone managed to get it right on the first try. In that final story, I look a little more closely at what it was that seemed to work. That's where the guidance comes in, as I suggest how you can try these techniques yourself if they make sense to you.

If any of this resonates with you, you've picked up the right book. Everything I'm going to discuss here was learned the hard way. Apparently that's my go-to style. I've had to learn some of these lessons the hard way multiple times, including some quite recently. I learned one again just yesterday, and regardless of when you read this book, I can guarantee that last statement is true. I continue to be a work in progress.

The stories you'll read in the following chapters draw from three key periods in my life: a pivotal year in Nicaragua when I was just 24, seven years as a community organizer in the Midwest, and almost two decades as a professional development coach. Today I'm the CEO of LeadQuine, an internationally recognized company challenging people to see *and be* a better version of themselves. My work with teams and individuals focuses on communicating more effectively, regardless of the circumstances.

If you're seeking perfection, you'll be disappointed. If you enjoy stories with a hint of humor, a little colorful language, and a lot of raw honesty, settle in, friend. Let's get started.

Chapter 1

ASSUMPTIONS AFFECT HOW WE SHOW UP

Let's start at the beginning and look at the first place where assumptions can enter our interactions: in new situations when we're meeting new people. We may feel inadequate, causing our self-confidence to take a nosedive. Our emotions can swing in the other direction, too, and create overconfidence based on a lack of awareness of ourselves and of others. Sometimes that overconfidence shows up as the "colonizer" attitude—one of superiority, like we're the first ones to have a great idea.

We struggle with how to show up the way we ideally want to in new situations because, well, they're new. We don't really know what to expect. Our past experiences might give some insights, but if it's truly a new situation or truly a new group of people, strategies that have worked well in the past may not apply. That's the point: we don't know.

But that doesn't mean there aren't some clear best practices to follow.

I wish I had known that 25 years ago.

Let the honest, soul-baring sharing begin.

Where you come from doesn't matter

On a spring evening in 1998, I walked into a meeting at Antioch Baptist Church in East Chicago, Indiana. I was with another community organizer, Emmett, who was more experienced but less outspoken than I was. I felt high on being newly hired to do the work I was sure I was meant to be doing.

There were a few church members waiting for us at a table in the meeting hall. They looked up at me and Emmett as we walked in. They greeted him warmly and eyed me warily. Emmett introduced me as we both sat down to begin the meeting.

I listened to the conversation about an upcoming community action the group was planning. Except that I wasn't really listening. I was trying to hear something I could latch onto and comment about that would establish my credibility. I felt a strong, driving urgency to prove myself and make sure everyone was glad I was at their table. (Horribly arrogant, I know. But honest.)

I finally latched onto something. One of the women described a neighborhood meeting she'd attended. I'd grown up attending neighborhood meetings with my parents in Detroit. This was my chance. I raised my hand to speak.

"I had a similar experience in Detroit growing up," I began. Everyone was staring at me. I chose to interpret their looks as interested and plowed ahead, describing a meeting that very closely matched the experience the woman had mentioned. I sat back when I finished, looking around expectantly. I was hoping for an indication of acceptance or maybe recognition that I had street cred. All I got were hard stares for a full minute.

Looking at Emmett, I watched a bead of sweat run down his face as he started trying to smooth the situation out. One of the women at the table raised her hand abruptly, cutting him off.

"What does this have to do with our situation?" she asked impatiently. "How does your experience in Detroit help us here in East Chicago?" She glared at me, frowning, and I was taken aback.

"I–I'm not sure," I stammered. "I guess I wanted you to know I've seen these meetings before." It sounded lame to my ears, too.

The woman continued glaring at me. "Detroit is not East Chicago," she said flatly. "And this is not your neighborhood. You are not here to save us."

I swallowed hard, my face burning. I looked around the table, finally looking at everyone in the group and seeing the expressions on their faces. I saw irritation, disgust, disappointment, and anger.

I really wish I could say I pulled back and apologized in that moment, but this is an honest book, so I won't lie. I didn't. I pushed back harder. I felt desperate to be seen as credible and couldn't see that the way to do that would've been to eat some humble pie. Instead, I ended up sounding whiny. I could hear it even then, and I cringe at the memory of it now.

I wanted to just be accepted. I grew up in Detroit and spent a year in Nicaragua, and I was a racial minority in both places. I assumed my experiences of being the "other" in those settings would just magically give me access to acceptance from those in this setting who were also often seen as "other" in their environment.

What I got was schooled. In front of the whole group. I was informed that my past experiences did not buy me credibility in the present. They didn't matter. What mattered was my current attitude and approach. They didn't care where I had come from. They cared about how I showed up, listened, asked questions to understand, and demonstrated respect.

It was a painful experience, and an important one. I've never forgotten how embarrassing it was to be called out like that. I've also never forgotten how right they were. At the time, it felt like a slap across the face. In retrospect, it was a firm hug, the kind designed to let you know you're loved *and* expected to do better.

The assumptions I made walking into the meeting at that church were arrogant and driven by low self-confidence.

I was desperate to prove my value and, frankly, just to feel like my experiences mattered. I was looking for that validation because I was drowning in a sea of negative self-talk. I had come into community organizing after a life-changing and destabilizing year in Nicaragua. While that experience had caused the powerful revelation that I needed to switch from work focused on science to work focused on people, it hadn't given me enough self-confidence to walk in doing it right on day one. Or even day 264.

Arrogance, overconfidence, and low confidence all create the same problems: a lack of self-awareness and a lack of awareness of others. I was so caught up in my determination to prove my worth in that meeting that I failed to pay attention to the other people in the room. I showed up with something to prove. Their voices, their experiences, their opinions and insights mattered to me only as a stepping-stone to get to my goal, which was to be seen. While I accomplished that, it came at a price. I was disrespectful and made a poor first impression that took years to fully overcome.

It also created wariness on their end. The next time I met with that group, I felt a distinct coolness coming from them. They later told me that they assumed I would come in with the same approach and became defensive to brace themselves for it. I don't blame them for that. Past behavior is often the best predictor of future behavior, as my wise wife often says. It meant I had to work a lot harder to demonstrate that I'd learned my lesson.

Low self-confidence plagued me for years. After realizing that my arrogant approach of having something to prove wasn't working, I retreated. I did a lot more listening. But there were still many moments when it overpowered me.

Speak up, even when your voice shakes

After I'd been working as a community organizer for about three years, I was invited to lead a workshop at National Leadership Training, or "Weeklong," as we referred to it. Weeklong was an intensive week of leadership training for leaders and prospective organizers from organizations all over the country in the Gamaliel Foundation network. It was quite an honor. I was one of the youngest organizers to be asked to lead a workshop. I walked into that room and was immediately gripped by a paralyzing conviction that I didn't belong there.

Looking around at the faces staring back at me, I realized they were all significantly older than I was. I felt like a kid who had put on her parent's suit to play at being a grown-up. I assumed they all had way more experience than me and couldn't understand why I was the one in front of the room. Sweat trickled down my back and I had trouble breathing. I stammered, spoke quietly, then too loudly. In my petrified and unconfident state, I missed many opportunities to engage the group in the kind of agitational and challenging session I'd been invited there to lead.

At the break, my boss met me in the staff room and ripped into me. "What the fuck was that about?" she spat at me. "What exactly happened to you in there?"

She glared at me, hands on her hips, anger almost visibly running through her small frame. I shrank back. Much to my horror and humiliation, I couldn't hold back my tears. My face felt hot with shame and embarrassment.

"I don't know," I managed. "They're all just so much older and more experienced than I am."

She glared at me for another moment, then leaned across the table and got very close to my face. Her voice was a low growl, but less like a predator and more like a protective mama lion. "You are the reigning expert on building teams, and you let those leaders get away with making you think they knew more about it than you do."

I kept my head down and just nodded. She was totally right. My entire approach in the two-hour session had been based on assumptions—that they had more experience than me; that I wasn't qualified or good enough; that I had nothing of value to offer; that they had it all figured out already.

She leaned back and stared at me until I looked up. "You are the reigning expert," she repeated, more softly this time. "Go back in there and get out of your head. Every last person in that room has something to learn from you and room to grow." She leaned closer again. "You speak up about your experience, even if your voice shakes."

I took a few deep breaths and collected myself before getting some water and walking the hallways for a few minutes, trying to pull myself together. I walked back to the training room and looked around. The faces looking back at me did not look impressed. Several looked skeptical. A couple seemed downright hostile. I decided I had nothing to lose. It couldn't possibly go any worse than it had in the first half.

I've always been at my best as a facilitator when I'm engaging with the participants, so I started by asking a question: "By show of hands, who feels like they've built a good team?" Half a dozen hands in the room went up right away. Starting with the most skeptical-looking man of the bunch, I pointed at him and said, "Tell me why you think your team is so great."

As he answered and I asked more questions, I forgot my nerves. I forgot how much older everyone was. Fully in the moment, I pushed back and challenged each person willing to engage with me about their obstacles to building good teams. I could feel the energy in the room rise and watched expressions changing from dubious and disinterested to eager and determined. It was a great session.

My assumptions nearly paralyzed me that day. They were about my own value (assumption: lacking), what I could add (assumption: not much), and how I could help the people in that training room (assumption: I couldn't). My boss saw what happened to me, but she didn't make an assumption about why it had happened. She asked. Directly, brutally, and bluntly. Once I gave her my answer, she used it to push me in the way I needed to be pushed. Had she not asked, she might've made an incorrect assumption about where the problem lay. Despite her clear frustration with my early performance that day, she didn't assume anything. She asked.

That's all it takes. That's the main lesson of this book. Ask.

Assumptions about culture

I graduated from college in 1995 with a degree in biology. After working for a year in a cytogenetics lab, I wasn't sure science was for me. But in 1997, I had an opportunity to work in field biology in rural Nicaragua, and it turned out to be one of the most enlightening years of my life.

But not because of the science.

Having turned 24 just a couple weeks after arriving, I was pretty sure I was invincible and could handle just about anything. I worked for a partnership between a local non-governmental organization (NGO) and the Presbytery of Lake Michigan, which is part of the Presbyterian Church USA. I'm not part of that church but had married into it, along with the opportunity to go on this big adventure.

Many people had been commissioned by their regional presbyteries to go to places all over the world to work in local organizations attending to various needs of the community. Before departing, everyone went through extensive training sessions to try to prepare for the experience. One piece of advice from those training sessions still sticks with me now, all these years later: "Remove your shoes when you enter a new place. You weren't the first one there."

Having visited the place we were going to live once before, I assumed I knew what to expect. I didn't speak Spanish, but there was a language school I was to go to, and everyone had been so friendly and nice when the delegation visited that I was sure it would be a breeze.

It wasn't.

One of the first things I noticed was a different attitude about time. When we arrived in the capital city, the director in charge of the partnership from the Nicaraguan main office told us to meet her the next morning at 8:00 a.m. We arrived right on time to find the offices completely empty, except for a woman cleaning who told us the director usually arrived between 9:00 and 9:30 a.m., along with the rest of the staff. We sat waiting, and when she arrived, we were introduced to *hora Nica*, which means "Nicaraguan time." We all laughed a little uncomfortably.

In the early days out in Nueva Guinea where we were living, I walked into a meeting already happening. Though I tried to slip in quietly and take a seat without disrupting things, all eyes turned to stare at me, and the meeting came to a halt. I flushed bright red, unclear about what I had done wrong. Unsure of what to do, I finally said, "Buenos días." Everyone in the group responded "Buenos días," and the meeting resumed.

I was informed afterward that walking into any room without giving the appropriate greeting is considered extremely bad manners. In my experiences in the US, it was bad manners to disrupt a meeting with a greeting. You waited for the right moment to apologize for being late. I had operated under the assumption that how things work in my culture would be universal. (Yes, the arrogance of that statement makes me cringe, too. But without honest reflection on our experiences, how do we learn?)

After a couple of exhausting and overwhelming weeks, I was thumbing through the packet of materials from our training. I came across that line I'd written down: "Remove your shoes when you enter a new place. You weren't the first one there." I had understood it intellectually when I'd heard it during the training, but reading it again, I realized I hadn't fully understood it until that moment. To enter someone's house and take off your shoes is a sign of respect. You don't want to track in whatever might be on your shoes. Literally *and* figuratively. Leave your shit outside the door. It's your shit, and it doesn't belong mucking up someone else's house.

And yet here I was, tracking my shit all over Nueva Guinea.

I assumed I had to be "useful," but I didn't really know how to do that yet.

I assumed the pace of life would be fast, as it was in the US, so I was putting a lot of pressure on myself to figure out my "usefulness."

I assumed if I didn't hurry up and figure out how to be "useful," I'd be criticized or asked to leave.

Slowly, the daily experiences I was having were picking away at those assumptions. Several people were so kind to me. I was overwhelmed by trying to learn the language, but no one wanted me to leave town for six weeks to go through the language course, including me. The more Spanish I picked up, the more insistent they became that I stay put and learn from them.

I finally realized I needed to "remove my shoes." I needed to stop putting all my own shit (expectations, assumptions, and projections) onto other people. I needed to take my damned shoes off and be humble.

I had to realize that I wasn't the first one there and listen to those who were.

I wish I could say I snapped my fingers, adjusted beautifully, and that everything from that point forward went really well. It didn't. But I did start remembering to mentally take my shoes off when I visited a new community or met a new group and leave my shit outside the door. I smiled a lot, listened a lot, and gave a lot of thought to how I was showing up. It went a long way toward helping me connect meaningfully with those around me.

Gradually, I let go of my assumptions about my own culture being universal and relaxed into the way of life in that region. I learned Spanish well enough to cause natives to do a double take and wonder if I was a light-skinned native. It was one of the hardest years of my life, and a great introduction to the importance of being aware of how my assumptions affected the ways I showed up.

An example of not guessing your way through it

Allow me to conclude this chapter with a story of someone who always seemed to show up the "right" way and assume nothing: the Reverend Cheryl Rivera.

The first time I met Rev. Rivera, she walked into the offices of the Interfaith Federation where I was a new community organizer sitting in a meeting. She was a powerful presence. She was impeccably dressed to the nines, with eyes that seemed to look right into your soul. She was quiet and unassuming, and her gaze never wavered. I was more than a little intimidated by her, and greatly in awe immediately.

The executive director, Paul, quickly made space at the head of the table and motioned Rev. Rivera to come sit there. She waved him away, barely taking her eyes off the person speaking, and took a chair on the outer edge of the group. She sat still, watching without seeming to blink, drinking in the words of the speaker.

When she did speak, it was to ask a few questions. She made no assumptions. She asked. This went on for several minutes. She never gave her own opinion or cut the other person off. She listened, asked, nodded her understanding, paused, and asked something else. I couldn't stop watching her.

Rev. Rivera had a way of getting others to speak without saying a word herself. She might ask a simple, open-ended question, or she might simply look at you, waiting for the absurdity or contradiction of something you'd just said to catch up with you.

Over the eight years that I worked with her in some capacity, I don't remember seeing her behave any differently. She isn't perfect; she'd be the first to say that. But refusing to make assumptions is one skill she seems to have perfected. I hope to be like her when I grow up.

What did she do that was so magical?

1. Whenever and wherever she showed up, she instinctively did so with tremendous awareness. She seemed to always be keenly aware of everyone present, as well

as of how her presence might impact the group. While staying tuned to her own inner voice, she focused on everyone else, watching reactions and facial expressions, reading body language, and paying attention at a level beyond casual. She matched her own responses to the mood in the group.

2. She asked a lot of questions yet never made us feel like we were being bombarded with them. The questions she asked were very often open-ended, leaving room for other opinions and ideas. She didn't make us feel like we were being interrogated but, instead, that she valued our insights and opinions and was simply trying to extract them from us.

3. She really listened. When she asked a question, she considered our answers thoughtfully before asking the next one or responding. She didn't hesitate to ask us to explain our point of view or why we felt the way we did. But it never felt demanding or intimidating. It felt like she was genuinely curious and interested.

I learned the hard way from the people at that church in the beginning of this chapter. It matters how you show up. First impressions really do last. When you get it wrong, it can take a very long time to change it. It requires effort to build a new impression with a person or group that aligns with what you're hoping to get across.

What motivated Rev. Rivera to consistently show up in the way she did? I've never asked her, but I can speculate. She was committed to proving she belonged at the table of decision-makers. She gave the impression of confidence, but I don't know how confident she actually felt. I suspect part of what fueled her questions was the desire to make sure she had all the information and didn't assume anything.

And that's another important thing to consider: what motivates you to engage rather than make assumptions? I can't speak for Rev. Rivera, but part of *my* motivation is making sure I'm perceived as being genuinely interested in the perspectives of others, open to their ideas, and willing to listen. What's yours?

Pausing to consider how you want to be perceived—before you enter into an interaction or a meeting—will help you. It gives you a moment to think, be intentional, and remember that there are other people involved. Their perspective matters. Mentally take your shoes off. You weren't the first one there.

Chapter 2

ASSUMPTIONS AFFECT HOW WELL WE READ OUR AUDIENCE

I t's common to experience some level of nervousness or anxiety when we know we have to make a presentation, sell something, or engage in any form of sharing our perspective. That nervousness tends to make us forget to pay attention to everyone else as we turn inward and focus on what we want to say or tell our audience. To compound the ineffectiveness of this kind of one-sided communication, we usually come into these situations with a boatload of assumptions.

We make assumptions about how much of the back story an audience needs.

We make assumptions about how much detail they need to understand the point we're making.

We make assumptions about what they need to know about us (for example, how smart we are).

When we get caught up in those assumptions, we forget to gauge our audience's interest and understanding throughout our communication. We forget to make sure we're bringing them along with us and that our points are landing with them as intended. We forget to pay attention to the cues they may be giving us.

We can't adjust our message or style based on cues if we aren't looking for them.

They want all the details

Years into my career in professional development, I joined an organization of coaches who focused on small business owners. I had been working with people long enough by that point to know better than to go into a meeting with something to prove. And yet, that's exactly what I did.

I'd never really had to "sell" my services before. In my work as a community organizer, institutions participated in *doing* the work before they invested in paying membership dues to the organization. The approach was very much "try before you buy." And community organizing lived in the nonprofit world, which just seemed so completely different from the business world. In my brain, working with small business owners was something totally new. You would've thought I had left all my training and experience in the car, considering the way I went into the meeting ready to conquer.

I met with a group of three people who were starting a marijuana growing business. They were smart, accomplished people but hadn't worked together before on this type of venture. They had an interest in learning how business coaching could help them better navigate any challenges they might face in their new operation. I had met with one of them previously, which is where the invitation to meet with the group had come from. But the moment she told me about this venture, my brain jumped straight to Assumption Land about what they must "need."

As the four of us sat down, I remembered my training and asked what they hoped to get from the meeting. One person said they wanted to learn more about business coaching to see if it was something that could help them. That answer was all the permission I needed, and my training went back out to the car.

I launched into a long presentation about business coaching and all the ways it could help their business. As I spoke, I noticed small shifts in their posture and possibly a couple of attempts to interrupt me. I spoke louder, faster, and with more animation, and I plowed on ahead.

At the end of my speech, I looked around expectantly, ready for someone to sign the contract. Two members of the group, including the one I had met with previously, were uncomfortably glancing at each other. The third was just staring at me. I tried to read her expression. She looked perplexed. I asked, "What other questions do you have?" She gave a sharp laugh.

"I think you've told us everything we need to know," she said, smiling at me with a warmth that didn't quite reach her eyes. "I think we just need some time to talk it over together, as business partners. Thanks so much for taking the time to meet with us today." And with that I was dismissed.

When I debriefed the meeting with my mentor, he did what I should've done in the meeting with the prospective clients. He asked me endless questions about how I had handled the meeting, why I had chosen the approach I had, and what the group had wanted. As he probed deeper into that last area, I realized I had no idea what they had wanted. As soon as I'd gotten the first invitation to tell them more about the program, I had stopped thinking about them. Instead, I had focused on making sure I covered all the features and benefits of our program, wanting not to forget any vital pieces of information. I had been sure it was just information they needed to be ready to move forward. At least, that's what I had assumed.

When I followed up with the group a few days later, they politely put me off. This continued for a few weeks, until I finally saw the original woman I'd met with at another function and asked her directly whether they'd made a decision. She told me sheepishly that they'd decided to try moving forward on their own for now but would "definitely call" if they ran into problems.

They never called back.

Assumptive emailing

Communicating based on assumptions—with all the damage they can do—isn't restricted to the spoken word.

Email is a breeding ground for assumptions. Without the give-and-take of a verbal conversation, we communicate only from our own perspective, which is often filled with assumptions.

We assume we know what information the recipient needs.

We assume our intent will be understood as intended.

We assume our tone will be correctly perceived.

How many times have you read an email from someone and not understood what they were asking for or what they were trying to say? How many times have you interpreted the "tone" of the email and taken offense or become defensive? How many times have you ended up being wrong about what the emailer actually intended to convey?

The problem is on both sides of the interaction. The writer is likely not taking the time to consider their audience and focus on what they need. Instead, the writer is focused on what they want to tell them. Sometimes they assume the recipient needs the entire back story to understand their point. Sometimes they assume the recipient needs no back story information at all to answer a question. And sometimes they simply haven't taken the time to stop and think about *what* the other person really needs to know and how to focus in on that.

One of the most annoying ways I've experienced this phenomenon is with LinkedIn InMail. My in-box, and I'm sure yours too, fills up with people trying to sell me their services. These messages are loaded with assumptions from beginning to end. There's no engagement with me as a unique individual, and there's no attempt to understand me or my business.

Salespeople have been selling from the beginning of time and will continue to do so. My complaint isn't with salespeople in general but with the offensiveness of the assumptions. I could share a dozen examples, but I'll just use one. This is a real message, copied verbatim, that arrived in my in-box recently:

"Hi Ellen, I am with a pay-per-performance marketing company. I came across LeadQuine and am pretty confident we can bring more business your way. Over the past 4 years, we have put 1000's of people into events & generated more than 30,000 leads for coaches, consultants & service-based businesses busy serving their clients. We know we can help your company grow."

Do you now? And how is that? What have you learned about my business that makes you think you can help me? What have you learned about my business that makes you think I'm not already doing this?

At the risk of just sounding mean and crotchety, here's my point about these messages: there are assumptions throughout them. I may be the face of my company, but that doesn't mean I'm new in business. That message is squarely targeting someone who is new to the industry and having trouble getting clients. If you've never spoken to me, how do you know whether that's *my* struggle? Maybe I'm struggling with something completely different.

The people who get responses from me are the ones who cite at least one thing about me they read on my page or my website. It demonstrates that some level of effort and thought went into contacting me. I also respond well to people who express uncertainty about whether their services will be a good fit for me. The "I'm not sure if we can help you" approach always makes me want to learn more.

"Wide-net" selling, which is premised on putting a whole bunch of invitations out there hoping a small percentage will accept, will always be with us, but must it continue to be filled with so many assumptions? Receiving an email that invites me to a conversation is much more appealing to me. Demonstrate curiosity. Ask questions. You're much more likely to get a response from me.

Who are you really focused on?

Presentations are great examples of places where assumptions take over if we're not paying attention. When we're presenting information, we become so focused on our goals, our agendas, and our needs that we can forget to pay attention to (or sometimes even consider) what the people we're talking to might want or need.

When teaching presentation skills to people, I often hear them say they are too nervous to pay attention to reading the room. Remember the story from chapter 1 about my disaster in the training room? Yeah, I've done it too. We become so focused on what we need to tell the audience that we simply can't shift the focus to what they might want or need out of the presentation.

A few years ago, I worked with an engineer we'll call "Raul" in a presentation skills workshop. After attending his first operations review meeting and presenting updates to the group on his projects, he came into our class saying simply, "I need help. My presentation didn't go well. I'm not sure what happened, but they were yelling at me by the end."

Having worked with many teams in manufacturing, I wasn't surprised by the yelling part. But I was curious about why it had happened, so I asked him to walk me through it.

Raul said that he had been a nervous wreck going into the meeting. He wasn't sure exactly what they wanted to hear in the presentation, so he crammed every detail imaginable about his projects onto 45 slides. He had 10 minutes to present.

He was so singularly focused on getting through all the material and telling them everything he thought they should know that he forgot to pay any attention at all to the reactions in the room. He admitted to noticing at one point that his boss was looking at him with a horrified expression. But rather than trying to understand why and what to do about it, Raul's response had been to turn slightly away from his boss and talk even faster.

Even after pulling these details out from his experience, I could tell Raul couldn't see what he had done wrong. And in my experience, Raul isn't exceptional in this way. We've all got some type of blinders on, and it often takes outside feedback to remove them. It was only after watching other people in the workshop present their topics that Raul began to see the problem. Some of the presenters had used the same style of forging blindly ahead that he had, and it clicked. He had to experience it to understand it.

The first assumption Raul made was the most damaging: his audience would need to know All The Things and he was there to prove that he knew All The Things. The second assumption, made during the presentation, was that he should just plow ahead and talk faster when he finally noticed some reaction (which was negative) from his audience.

Raul fell into the trap of believing that if he could just get through all his material, his audience would understand everything and think he was brilliant. I fell into the same trap in my meeting with the group of marijuana growers I described at the beginning of this chapter. Switching gears when you've prepared material can be terrifying. Or at least irritating. But we have to do it anyway or risk being ineffective at best or disrespectful of our audience at worst.

What can you do in the moment? Simply stop talking. You can tell your audience that you want to make sure you're giving them the information they need, then ask them whether there are any gaps you need to fill before you move on. It's a simple check-in along the way. When I suggested this to Raul as a strategy he might try, he stared at me with an expression of mild horror on his face. I asked him what was wrong.

"But what if they totally derail my presentation and take it in a completely different direction than what I prepared for?" he said with obvious panic on his face.

"What if they do?" I replied. "What's the worst that can happen?"

Raul thought for a moment and decided it might be worth a try. He worried that the presentation would go in a different direction than what he'd prepared for, but if the topic was still his projects, he realized he would be able to answer most of the questions they could ask him.

When we don't check in with our audience, whether we're talking to just one person or a room of 100, we risk continuing in the wrong direction with our presentation. Just because we successfully say All The Things doesn't mean we're providing value for those who are listening. Presenting material that isn't useful to your audience wastes not only their time but also yours. Be courageous. Be willing to check in. The new conversation may be more useful for everyone.

An example of not guessing your way through it

Before everything shut down in 2020 due to the COVID-19 pandemic, the last workshop I facilitated was with a manufacturing plant team in California. I had worked with most members of this team in previous workshops, but they had moved a few people around since then. This current group was struggling as a new team.

The director overseeing the group asked me to put together a workshop focused on helping them gel better as a team. The plant manager was struggling to get the team to perform because of a lack of trust. The director told me what he felt were the critical topics to cover, and I put the three-day workshop together.

The first day went fairly well. The group members (I wouldn't have called them a team at that point) were all engaged, but it was easy to see the distrust among them. Most everyone was very polite. When one guy did push back at me on a couple things, I had the distinct impression it had nothing to do with me. He was aiming his frustration at me simply because he was unable to direct it at those for whom it was intended.

At the end of the day, I sat with the director, his vice president (VP), and another upper-level corporate manager. We talked about how the day had gone. I shared my observations of the group and the tension I was sensing. The VP agreed with me that we needed to address it or it could become a bigger problem. The director wasn't convinced, but he agreed to pay attention to it the following day and was willing to let me adjust course if I needed to.

As we got into the second day, I became more and more convinced that the topics I'd prepared were not going to get this group where they needed to be. I sensed subtle jockeying for position taking place in the room. Too much was being left unsaid. Tension between certain individuals was starting to build and become obvious.

At a break, I touched base with the director and the VP, telling them that we needed to abandon the planned material and help the group get into a real discussion. The director was still hesitant to change course. He really wanted the group to address the topics he had identified. I pointed out that they'd get nothing out of those topics if we didn't address the elephant in the room. The VP backed me up and, finally, the director agreed.

I called the group back from break and turned off my PowerPoint. Grabbing a flip chart and marker, I said, "Let's change gears. I'm sensing some tension in the room, and I think we might need to have a different conversation before we can effectively move forward with other topics."

As I spoke, I watched the reactions of the group members. Some were nodding at me, and others showed relief on their faces. On other faces I observed anxiety. On the plant manager's face, there was surprise and mild annoyance. I decided to let the majority rule.

In my role as facilitator, I was able to set the stage for the group to start talking and then sit back and watch how they interacted. When someone would make an assumption and I saw someone else react negatively to it, I'd stop the conversation and make space for them to clear it up. When I could see the room reacting negatively to someone's assertion or position, I'd stop them and ask the room to give voice to the eye-rolling and arm-crossing they were doing.

It was a difficult couple of hours, but once they realized I wasn't going to move on with the prepared material until they were willing to engage with each other and clear the air, they did the work. The result was so much better than it would've been if I'd simply plowed ahead with my prepared agenda.

At the end of the day, I sat down again with the same group of leaders. The VP and the director agreed we had done the right thing.

Sometimes we're too committed to the direction we've planned to be willing to adjust, as I was with my sales pitch to the business owners I described at the beginning of this chapter. But if we're really focused on the people we're trying to engage, we can get it right. In this case, I read the room and asked questions instead of plowing ahead. How would your next presentation be improved if you did the same?

It can be challenging to figure out how to plan for this type of check-in and engagement with your audience. Here are a few questions you can ask yourself when preparing your presentation to make sure your audience is your focus:

- What are the expectations of the presentation?
- What outcome(s) is/are expected?
- Who will be there?
- What do they know about the topic already?
- What would be most important to share?

The answers to these questions might elicit additional clarifying questions. You can use them to help you prepare for any presentation, whether talking to one person or presenting to an audience of many. We damage our credibility when our message misses the mark. It doesn't make us look better to simply tell more. It just makes an ass out of you and me.

Chapter 3

ASSUMPTIONS AFFECT THE
SUCCESS OF MEETINGS

Meetings in and of themselves are not toxic. They can be a wonderful opportunity to bring several smart people into one space to brainstorm, problem-solve, create a plan of action, and collaborate. What *can* become toxic is the culture that develops around meetings.

In many organizations I've worked with over the years, meetings have become the place where the energy in a team goes to die. They turn into a time to wax eloquent and show how smart people are through soapboxing or getting into a pissing contest with another participant. The meetings have no clear objectives or outcomes, so they meander and go on too long. They often end only because the participants have another meeting to go to and not because anything has been resolved or advanced. They can also be a prime breeding ground for assumptions.

We make assumptions about the time participants have to give to a meeting.

We make assumptions about who's responsible for the success of the meeting.

We make assumptions about the purpose and goal of the meeting.

Assumptions run wild in meeting culture, turning it toxic. The "not my job" mentality removes any possibility of making it better. We must be willing to find ways to speak up, help get things back on track when they go off the rails, and turn each meeting into an experience that helps our teams rather than hurts their productivity and spirits.

"My agenda is the most important one"

Managers and leaders everywhere can easily fall into the trap of thinking their agenda is the most important one. I coached several directors on an executive team who all spoke regularly about how their boss, the CEO, did this. He would schedule a weekly meeting of the full team to run for 90 minutes.

Frequently, one of the leaders I was coaching would message me from the meeting to say they weren't going to make our session because they were still in the meeting, four hours later. The CEO's baseline assumption seemed to be that his meeting was the most important thing on everyone's calendars for that day. He also seemed to assume that running over the scheduled time was perfectly acceptable. If someone spoke up that they had another meeting, he shamed them in front of the whole team for daring to schedule something "so close" to his meeting.

This happened once to one of the leaders I coached. The boss's meeting was supposed to run from 9:30–11:00 a.m. The leader's next meeting was at 2:00 p.m., and when they spoke up at 1:45 p.m. to bow out of the boss's meeting, the boss called the leader on the carpet.

When I asked each of the leaders separately what went on in these meetings, they all said the same things: The agenda was packed full of reporting. The boss had nine people directly reporting to him, and each of them had a slot on the agenda to report on what their team was working on. As they reported, the boss would ask questions about the details to a degree that none of them felt was productive at that level of the organization. He would at times pick apart a single report done by an entry-level analyst, challenging the department director who was two levels above that analyst about how to rewrite sections of it.

When I asked if this agenda was helpful to them, they all said no. But to push back and suggest something different to the CEO wasn't an option any of them would consider at the time. He had trained them to be afraid of his verbal assaults and convinced them that he was just a lot smarter than they were. They all worried they'd lose their jobs if they dared to question his methods.

After I'd been coaching other leaders in the organization for about a year, the CEO asked me to coach him for a six-month engagement. He was frustrated on his side of the desk about what he perceived to be a lack of engagement from his directors. From his perspective, they should've been pushing back more. He claimed to want to be challenged and felt they were all too weak to stand up for their ideas, but he couldn't see how his treatment of them contributed to their unwillingness to push back.

He also couldn't see the assumptions he was making as problematic. He simply felt he was right. Leaders in positions of power must be careful with this thinking. Being able to command your team's time doesn't mean you should assume your agenda is the only one of importance. If what you want to build is a team of leaders who can truly help you run your organization more effectively, there has to be more give-and-take. There also must be a stronger baseline of mutual respect.

Through the coaching work we did together, the CEO became a little more willing to ask for rather than demand more time if his meetings ran long. He's restructured the organization to have fewer direct reports, which seems to be helping. The directors have also become a little more willing to speak up and have each other's backs in these meetings. It's not perfect, but it's progress.

If you schedule it, they will come

One company I've worked with for a few years now is famous for holding conference calls. This company has production plants in several states, so meeting in person with each other on a regular basis isn't practical. The VPs over various areas of operation hold these calls, and the invitations to the calls go out to very long lists of people. It's a wide-net approach. If everyone is invited, no one can say they weren't in the loop.

There seems to be a clear expectation and assumption that everyone who's invited will be on the call. Very often there's no clear agenda or understood purpose to the meetings. The leaders and team members who've been invited feel a tremendous amount of frustration about this, but no one feels it's their place to push back. The people invited to the call feel an obligation to keep showing up for such calls because they fear that the one call they decide to skip will be the one during which something critical happens. There are also far too many people on the calls for the meetings to be productive. Even if they had a focused agenda, discussion could only be very limited with that many people involved.

The consistent problem across these examples is the lack of accountability on the part of the meeting chair. No one is challenging the chair of the meeting to do something different. The chair either doesn't know how to do things better or simply doesn't care to do something different. They may think their methodology is perfectly acceptable. After all, people keep showing up when they receive the meeting invites, so the chair assumes that all must be well with the way they plan and conduct the meetings.

It's not. Meeting chairs have a responsibility to design meetings with their participants in mind. And not having clear objectives or outcomes is simply unacceptable.

Because there's a power imbalance between leaders and their subordinates, meetings called by leaders are difficult to ignore. Often, those invited to such meetings feel powerless to ask questions that could help improve the outcomes and quality of the meeting because of this power imbalance. Ineffective meeting habits are so ingrained in many organizations that people are simply resigned to accepting them. However, when I start asking questions about it, the frustration and desire for something different come pouring out.

When we design meetings with our participants in mind, we bring focus, clarity, and purpose to the meetings. Why gather all those brilliant minds in one place if we aren't going to use them? If we're not interested in getting engagement from the participants in a meeting, we don't need a meeting, we need an email.

Who's responsible for the success of the meeting?

Nothing sends people reverting to "not my job" thinking like a meeting. The inherent assumption is that the chair of the meeting is the only one responsible for the success of the meeting. "Well, it's not my meeting." Hmm…

Sure, the responsibility for putting a good meeting together is primarily that of the chair. But once that meeting invitation goes out, the assumptions run wild regarding what happens from there.

The person receiving the invitation assumes they have been invited because their presence has been carefully considered and is essential. Maybe. Or they could've been invited because the chair was covering their bases by using a wide-net approach. The person's name is on a list somewhere, so they got thrown into the mix.

Rather than assuming we must attend and getting annoyed before the meeting even starts, we could ask some questions. "I appreciate you including me in the meeting invite. I'm not sure I totally understand how I might contribute. Can you help me see why you think my participation would be beneficial to the group?"

Once the meeting begins, the assumption of ownership and responsibility is projected squarely onto the meeting chair. It happens so often that when it doesn't, it's the exception. One director I coach, for example, leads a team of seven. They are all responsible for other teams of people carrying out the main business of this company. Each of them is used to overseeing their teams, and are good, solid leaders. But they weren't acting like it when they came to their director's meetings.

The director was frustrated at the team's lack of engagement in her weekly meetings. She asked me to come observe a meeting with them to determine whether I could help her see what she was missing. I agreed and attended the next regular weekly meeting. We stipulated that she would prepare the agenda as she usually did, and I would attend only to observe and give feedback at the end.

She sent the agenda out the day before the meeting, which was great. However, I immediately noticed some potential problems with how it was structured. She was using it in part for information sharing, and the team members were all a little bored with that practice, including her. She also didn't have anything timed on the agenda. Nothing was creating any sense of urgency to keep the meeting moving.

But during the meeting, I noticed something interesting as I watched the group. While one person was reporting on their team activities, a few were checking email or doing other work. Several people sat back in their chairs and had their arms folded. One man checked his watch repeatedly. They were not only disengaged but weren't even listening.

I didn't interrupt the meeting but watched the whole painful thing play out. At the end, I asked the group if they would stay for a few minutes to debrief. The director had ended the meeting a few minutes early to give me time to do that without disrupting their schedules, so they could hardly say no. But no one looked excited about it.

Although it took some prodding and encouragement from the director, as well as assurances that there would be more negative repercussions for holding back than for honesty, we finally got the members of the group to admit they were frustrated with the meetings. When I probed more into what specifically was bothering them, they cited how the meeting was organized. They didn't find value in listening to updates from each other. They didn't like it when discussions went off topic and got into the weeds on something unrelated to the main focus of the meeting.

The director was taking notes, trying to be open to hearing their feedback. I applauded her willingness to hear it, but something else wasn't sitting right.

"Why didn't any of you speak up in the meeting about these frustrations?" I asked. Silence. Eight pairs of eyes stared at me, unsure how to respond. After a few seconds, one of the men spoke up.

"It's not our meeting. It's hers."

Oof. That's the underlying assumption that's poisoning meeting culture everywhere. "Not my job."

Why was he willing to waste his time like that? Why sit through an unproductive meeting? Are there medals being handed out somewhere for the team's tolerance of wasted time? I call bullshit.

If we switch to an assumption that the success of the meeting is the responsibility of everyone in attendance, how would things shift?

I asked this team that question. After some thinking and discussion, they decided there were clear ways they could speak up during a meeting that would still be respectful of their director. They came to see that it was possible to interrupt from a place of good intention, support, and commitment to the outcome and decided to practice at their next meeting.

Over time, things began to improve. They still slip into old habits occasionally. They also admit it's much harder to sit through other meetings where they don't have as much at stake. But they don't speak up about it because it feels like swimming upstream. They have chosen to engage at that level with their director, but they don't consistently feel like the risk of speaking up is worth it in all meetings quite yet.

Change is hard. But if we keep working at it, it doesn't have to be someone else's job.

An example of not guessing your way through it

The organization I worked for as a community organizer was a coalition of churches and community organizations working together on issues of metropolitan equity. The central question our work sought to answer was, "What is getting built where, and for whose benefit?" Most of the time the answer didn't favor older cities and suburbs. Urban sprawl was at an all-time high at that point, and the inner cities and older suburbs were dying.

Everyday working people who were part of the neighborhood churches saw what was happening and knew it wasn't in alignment with their core values. When we were able to tap into that misalignment, people were willing to mobilize into action. A huge part of my job was building relationships to understand the full picture, see possibilities for taking action, and challenge people to organize for change.

As I developed relationships with hundreds of church members and leaders, I helped them build what we called Core Teams in every church within our organization. Leaders from different churches would meet one another if they worked on an organization-wide task force together, but otherwise they were mostly siloed from each other. The Core Teams weren't learning best practices from each other, sharing information, or challenging each other. It was a huge missed opportunity for growth. A few of the organization's leaders decided we should change that, so we created the Core Team Assembly.

The Core Team Assembly was made up of two representatives from each Core Team, but all members were welcome to attend. The purpose of the group was clear from the beginning: create a place for Core Teams to learn from each other's best practices, train together on relevant topics, and hold each other accountable for continuously developing the base of the organization.

I learned about meeting culture first as an organizer. From the national level down to the local, we were very strict on creating and following tight agendas. We knew that we were asking busy people who worked full time, had families, and were active in their churches and communities to be part of the organization. They wouldn't tolerate wasting time with meeting for the sake of meeting.

We limited the number of topics we would address at any given meeting to three. If there were more than the allotted three, the representatives voted on which ones were the top priorities. Other topics got moved to other committees to handle or were tabled until the next assembly. If someone had an update to give, there was a deadline by which it had to be submitted ahead of time via email. It made it onto the agenda only if there was an action item associated with it. Otherwise, it was entered into the report from the meeting as information. We also designated two timekeepers at each meeting to make sure the meeting kept moving. They worked together to make sure we stayed on track and gave each other courage to interrupt if need be. It worked incredibly well.

The decisions we made about how to run those meetings were grounded in what we knew people expected out of those meetings, not based on assumptions. We knew they didn't want us to waste their time because they told us. We knew what they valued because we asked for feedback at the end of every meeting.

The practices we employed as community organizers and leaders are not far-fetched. They absolutely apply in your boardroom or staff meeting. The best way to avoid creating a meeting built on incorrect assumptions about what the right agenda would be is to stop and ask yourself a series of questions like the ones below. These questions are designed to help you reflect on the meeting participants. When you do that, you position yourself to design a meeting that people want to be part of because the value is clear to them.

- Who are the participants in terms of their relationship to you?
- What is the purpose of this meeting? Are you brainstorming? Making decisions? Creating a plan? Reaching agreement?
- Why do participants think they are coming to this meeting?

- What are the participants' starting points? What beliefs, biases, attitudes, priorities, fears, or assumptions might they bring?

Once you understand how and why your participants are showing up for a meeting, you're in a better position to design the meeting to create connections and accomplish your goals. But you can't stop there. Now you need the right agenda. Here are six steps for creating an agenda that will lead to a clear, concise, and effective meeting:

1. *Set clear objectives.* What's the purpose of the meeting? What outcome are you trying to reach? Could this be done by email, or does it require group thinking or action?
2. *Set clear time limits.* The overall meeting time should be set and respected. Each segment of the agenda should also be timed. If you don't use time limits for specific agenda items, you risk letting the meeting wander unproductively.
3. *Assign roles.* You're probably chairing this meeting if you're designing the agenda. But are there agenda items that should or could be led by other people? Who will summarize the next steps at the end of the meeting? Ask at least one person to be a timekeeper. If this is a new practice and the timekeeper recruit might have trouble interrupting as needed, ask two people to do this job together.
4. *Plan for engagement.* Yep, plan for it. How do you want people to participate? How will you achieve this?

Preplan questions designed to engage. Make space for them in your timed agenda. Send out the agenda and the questions to participants ahead of time so they can give some thought to their answers.

5. *Do not leave the meeting without summarizing.* Who will do what by when? Are there any next steps or actions? Is there a next meeting?

6. *Ask for feedback.* How will you get feedback on the meeting from the participants? How will you know whether it was worth their time? How will you know where you can improve next time?

Meeting assumptions and the damage they can do can be avoided with a little effort beforehand. Shift your perspective away from how much you want to tell people when they gather for your meeting. Focus instead on what they need. You just might find that your team has a lot more to offer than you assumed.

Chapter 4

ASSUMPTIONS AFFECT WHAT QUESTIONS WE ASK (AND HOW WE ASK THEM)

Asking questions can be challenging, especially for those to whom it doesn't come naturally. It can cause anxiety as they wonder whether the question they want to ask is going to create a conflict or problem for others. Even for those who are naturals at asking questions, it can take some effort to make sure they're doing it in a way that enables their audience to really hear them. One way to begin is to internally question ourselves (and our assumptions) before externally asking questions of others.

Assumptions directly dictate the kind of questions we ask, how we ask them, and whether we ask them. Our assumptions are often built into the way we formulate our questions. We may be assuming things about the answers, what the other person is willing to share, or whether the other person will correctly interpret the tone of the question.

We don't take enough responsibility for carefully crafting the "right" questions.

The ones that don't have any assumptions built into them.

The courageous ones.

The ones we don't already know the answers to.

We can't just ask *more* questions. We need to ask the *right* questions.

Not a natural

Years ago, before becoming certified as a professional executive coach, I was working with a client on several leadership development workshops. The workshops focused primarily on presentation skills, but I had also facilitated a handful of workshops with teams in the organization that were focused on specific communication challenges each team was experiencing. Those workshops had gone reasonably well, and the client asked if I would begin coaching a few of the team leaders.

I happily accepted, though with a tiny bit of trepidation. The extent of my "training" to coach a leader was virtually nonexistent at that point, but as a community organizer, I had worked one-on-one with plenty of leaders in some sort of unofficial mentoring role. The interactions had been focused on challenging and supporting them to reach a specific, targeted goal related to their work. It sounded about the same as what this client was asking. How hard could it be?

I made mistake number one before I even took on the engagement.

Oscar was one of the team leaders. He had been through my presentation skills workshop and participated in two of the more focused workshops with his team. He was a pretty laid-back guy, and I was happy to coach him. I assumed he would feel the same way (mistake number two), so I jumped right in on our first call.

I laid out the very general things the HR director had shared with me about Oscar's challenges. When I asked if he had anything he wanted to add to the list, he said no. I suggested (mistake number three) we begin with time management. I felt most comfortable with that topic and was pretty sure I could provide solutions for him. Oscar didn't complain, which I took as a green light (I'll stop pointing out the mistakes now; I'm sure you get the idea).

We spent the first three sessions talking about time management. At the beginning of the fourth session, I asked Oscar how he thought the coaching was going. He hesitated slightly and then said he thought it was going fine. I then asked if there was something he wanted to do differently. He hesitated again and then said he wondered if we could talk about a different challenge, which he named. This challenge wasn't on the HR director's list, but I told him that although I thought there was still more to discuss about time management, we could talk about anything he wanted.

Oscar proceeded to tell me that he wanted to discuss one of his team members who wasn't performing up to standard. He asked how to get her to reengage and perform better, and I started making suggestions. (In case you're not familiar with it, this isn't how coaching works.) I did ask some questions along the way, but they were mostly about the logistics of the challenge he was having. I gave stellar, clever advice filled with steps he should take—and more assumptions than I can count.

When I first spoke to Oscar, I assumed I knew enough about him from our other workshop interactions to understand him. I assumed he was excited to be coached. I assumed the challenges and goals as explained by the HR director were the right starting point. I assumed coaching was really advising and that Oscar just wanted me to tell him what he should do. I assumed Oscar understood how coaching worked and also that he was coachable. Actually, that last part isn't true. I didn't even know being coachable was a thing at that point. I assumed everyone was coachable with the right coach.

In the coaching sessions themselves, I made loads of assumptions. There are literally too many to list. One of the first assumptions was that I should pick the topic for our discussion. On the heels of that one came the assumption that I knew what Oscar believed was the challenge with his time management. I thought I was being helpful by cutting to the chase and offering solutions.

What I've since learned the hard way, several times over, is that people are most likely to embrace the solutions they develop themselves. The job of anyone trying to coach others is to leave all assumptions at the door and ask the questions that help further their thinking to get them to the solutions. This is true whether your title is "coach" or you're simply engaging with a colleague or team member—or, really, anyone in your life.

When the HR director asked me to coach Oscar, I clarified with her all the logistics of the arrangement. How long did she want me to coach him? What were the main challenges and concerns leading her to seek coaching for him? What financial investment in coaching was she prepared to make? But here are the other questions I should've asked:

- What did *Oscar* want?
- Why was coaching the solution that the HR director felt would provide the best results?
- What outcomes was the HR director hoping for or expecting?
- What benchmarks would the HR director be looking for to help her know whether we were successful or not?
- Could I talk to Oscar before confirming that I would work with him?

Asking more questions isn't always enough. We need to ask *better* questions. When we don't, assumptions take over.

Asking the wrong questions, or the right questions the wrong way, can lead to many challenges. The way questions are constructed matters. It determines how our audience hears the questions. That determines how our questions make them feel. And that determines how they will respond.

Asking everyone except the one who can answer

Early on in running my own business, I started doing quite a bit of contracting work with another company. The CEO, who we'll call Driver, had a fantastic lead magnet system set up. The prospects looking for workshops like his came to him through the marketing and advertising campaigns he ran. There was never any cold calling or prospecting. It was heavenly for someone like me who detests the prospecting process.

Despite how much I liked the way contracting for him was set up, Driver and I had butted heads a few times over differences in our styles and approaches, both in conducting the sales process and in delivering workshops. Driver primarily trained me to deliver the workshops, so we saw a lot of each other in the first six months. But after my initial training period was over, our paths didn't cross all that often. He lived in Texas, and I was in Michigan.

I settled into the work and was quite happy with the autonomy I had. I was able to work from home, responding to incoming leads. If I closed a sale on a program, I traveled to deliver the program myself. The commission structure and my success rate were making me a nice living.

About two years into my contracting relationship with this company, Driver decided to change the commission structure. I was instantly furious. Before he could explain his reasons for the change to any of us who were contracting for him, I started calling my fellow contractors to ask them what they knew. We collectively bitched up a storm about how dumb the whole idea seemed and how unfair the new structure appeared to be to those doing the traveling and workshop delivery.

I didn't call Driver. He was the CEO. Even though I was a contractor, I still viewed him as The Boss, so I assumed there would be consequences for directly challenging him. I also assumed I wouldn't like what he had to say. Instead, I stomped around my condo for nearly a week, angrily assuming Driver was out to hurt all of us in order to preserve more wealth for himself, and bitterly complaining about it to anyone who would listen.

The following Monday on our weekly conference call, Driver laid out the commission structure in more detail. He talked about why he had decided to change it. He talked about the ways he thought everyone would benefit, regardless of their role with the company. He shared more details about how it would work in practice. Much to my surprise, it actually made sense. Despite how much I'd had to say to other people before the conference call, I was silent on the call itself.

I felt sheepish after it ended. A minute later, my phone rang. It was Driver. He had heard through the grapevine how upset I'd been and asked me why I hadn't just called him to talk about it. I didn't have a good answer.

I apologized for not coming directly to him with my questions and concerns.

My initial response to Driver's policy change had been influenced by my past experiences with him. We had disagreed several times about other things, and those experiences had made me suspicious and immediately skeptical regarding the commission structure change. That's quite often the case. Feelings about another person that stem from past experiences with them absolutely contribute to how we respond to them in new interactions. They affect how (and if) we craft the questions we're asking them.

In this case, not only did Driver and I have a history of past disagreements, but he was The Boss. I hadn't been sure if approaching him directly would cause him to rethink my value to his company. I hadn't wanted to be dismissed as a contractor. The fear of retribution or consequences of any kind is another common factor in how (and if) we decide to engage someone who has firing power over us.

How we ask questions matters. When we summon the courage to question The Boss, it's important to take an approach that's respectful. Apparently, I still had some lessons to learn about that after leaving Driver's organization and moving on to a new place.

Asking questions the wrong way got me fired

I was hired several years ago to work at a well-known hospital and medical school to help support diversity, equity, and inclusion work. The director of the office was a well-respected doctor from the hospital who had a passion for and track record in diversity, equity, and inclusion work. She had never led an organization like this before. But I had.

The director told me that part of why she was hiring me was because they wanted an outside perspective, meaning someone who hadn't already been working within the hospital or medical school system. I took that seriously, but with way too many assumptions built in.

My first assumption was that questions were welcome. My job description included creating my own job description. I didn't know what I didn't know, but I did know I needed to be able to meet lots of people and ask lots of questions in order to get ideas about how exactly I could be useful. When the green light to start reaching out to leaders in the institution wasn't forthcoming from the director, I asked her questions. In response, she'd usually stare at me with what looked like an obvious attempt to remain calm. Then she'd tell me to be patient.

Another assumption I made was that the director wanted to hear my outside perspective, knowing that I'd been an executive director of a large metropolitan organization. Because of this previous job, I had some experience with the challenges she faced in launching the work of this office.

In staff meetings, the director would present ideas and ask for input. I would hang back, waiting to see what other people would offer, which usually turned out to be a few polite, tentative comments. I assumed this was because they weren't sure what to say or hadn't done something like this before. So I jumped in. My suggestions or ideas were usually met with silence around the table. I wasn't exactly sure why. I assumed I had somehow stepped out of line or that my ideas were way off the mark in a way that I couldn't see. Either way, I didn't ask, and no one offered insight.

My fatal mistake came in a staff meeting during which the director laid out an idea for a campaign. I had run something very similar before, and I could see places where she might get into trouble. Assuming she hadn't thought it all the way through, I dove right in when she asked for input.

I asked if she had thought about alternate possibilities. I asked if she was planning on doing such and such. I asked questions in a way that, in hindsight, made it clear I didn't think she knew what she was doing. I didn't have malicious intent in that moment, but I also wasn't focused on the right thing, which was gaining a better understanding of her idea. Instead, I was using questions in a way that I now realize must've felt to her like a frontal assault on her idea.

After nine weeks, the director had had enough. My supervisor—to whom I reported technically but had never reported in reality—called me into the conference room and dismissed me. I was completely blindsided. There had been no warning, no conversation, no nothing leading me to believe I was walking some sort of fine line. The reason given in the letter I was asked to read and sign was that I had "failed to embrace The Way" of the institution.

I didn't even know what that meant. I tried to point out that one of the reasons highlighted for hiring me had been my outside perspective, which meant I didn't know "The Way" of the institution.

It didn't matter. I had to clean out my desk and was escorted out. It was one of the most humiliating experiences of my life.

It turned out that this director ended up dismissing 10 staff members in the course of 13 months and was investigated by the institution. She was ultimately dismissed herself. So I don't think my own dismissal was 100 percent due to my asking the wrong questions. But I do think there's an important point in that experience to be shared.

I'm betting I made the director feel insecure and less confident by the *way* I asked questions. My experience in this arena may have caused me to behave with a level of confidence and passion that was unsettling to her. The hierarchy in that institution is deeply ingrained, particularly among medical staff. I was a peon by comparison, with just a mere bachelor of arts degree. Who the hell was I to question a doctor? That medical hierarchy meant there was no way that director could allow herself to be seen as not having all the answers.

I don't accept responsibility for her stuff, but I do accept responsibility for the role I played. If I had stopped to reflect on the dynamics of my environment, I would've seen that she was struggling. I could've crafted questions that might've helped her think through the possible challenges, without putting her on the defensive.

An example of not guessing your way through it

One of the first people I was encouraged to meet with one-on-one as a young community organizer was "Big Mike" Koharchik. When I called him to set up the meeting, he told me in his deep, booming voice that he didn't know why I would want to come talk to him, because he had done all he was going to do.

Big Mike had been a central figure in the organization's campaign to get a federal courthouse seated in Gary, Indiana. Although it had taken years, he hadn't stopped fighting until he attended a ribbon-cutting ceremony on the steps of the new courthouse. He was a legend in the organization because of his tenacity and salt-of-the-earth demeanor. My boss wanted me to meet him because he didn't agree with Big Mike's declaration that he was all done working in his community.

I convinced Big Mike to meet with me, promising to not ask him to do a single thing other than tell me his story. Begrudgingly, and not without a few mild threats, he agreed. I was a little nervous but not seriously concerned. I had met people like Big Mike before. They have a whole lot of bark and bluster hiding a heart too big to look the other way when someone is in need.

Big Mike's physique matched his voice. He was in his Mid-60s by then, with snow-white hair. He stood well over six feet tall, with substance to his frame. He wasn't heavy, but working for decades in a cement plant had given him a solid build. He towered over me, emphasizing his height, which I think was a little bit on purpose. I tried not to smile.

As he sat down at his kitchen table while his wife quietly made coffee at the counter, he reiterated that he was all done being active in the community. I nodded and held up my hands in surrender. I wasn't there to do anything but get to know him a little bit and was prepared to honor the terms of his agreement to meet with me.

I started asking questions about his life, his passions, his family, and his role in getting the courthouse built. He relaxed as the conversation went on. He told me about his twin boys and the festival of twins in Ohio they'd visited every year when the boys were growing up. He told me many other stories about his life as well.

Toward the end of our conversation, I asked him what he saw happening at that time in his community. He looked at me sharply, silently warning me just with his frown not to ask him to do anything. I gazed back at him innocently and held my hands up again. "What?" I said. "I'm just asking what you see. I'm not asking you to do a damned thing!"

He hesitated, and then started describing what he was noticing in his neighborhood. There was no place for people of all ages to gather and engage in recreational activities. Kids were wandering around when they could be going to play organized sports. Older retired people in his church needed somewhere to go and have more social interaction.

When he finished, I thanked him for allowing me to get to know him a little bit, and I stood to leave. He looked at me, surprised. "You're not going to ask me to do anything?"

"You almost sound disappointed, Mike," I replied. "But I told you several times. I did not come here today to ask you to do anything except share your story with me. You've done that, and now I'm going to leave." I paused, reading the mild disappointment on his face. My boss had been right; this man was not done yet. If he didn't find something to do, he would accelerate his own death out of boredom.

"But ..." I began, hesitating, "if you want to talk again sometime ..." I let the comment hang.

He barely suppressed a smile and shrugged, trying to be nonchalant. "Maybe, kid," he said.

I smiled without hiding it and nodded, telling him I'd be in touch with his permission, and I took my leave.

My agenda that day had been all about Big Mike. I wanted to hear his stories, understand his perspective and insights, and see what he could see. I deliberately approached our interaction without any intention of getting him to do anything other than tell me those stories. Because I stayed focused on that goal, Big Mike trusted me. I asked the right questions. I made no assumptions.

How well do you know the people you work with? Beyond the superficial stuff, I mean. What do you know about the path they've walked to get to where they are and where they want to end up?

According to what we hear from our clients, it's pretty common for people to just know as much as they need to in order to direct team members to The Next Thing. We live very close to what's right in front of us. How can we meet the next deadline? Who will deliver that piece of the project? Did I get that update submitted on time? Will we make shipment?

These are critical, urgent questions that we need to be able to answer (or get answered) to check the boxes for delivering on whatever projects or metrics we're accountable to. But it's far from the full picture. We may have the "urgent" covered, but what about the "important"?

Each member of your team brings unique strengths, limitations, insights, and perspectives to the table. If you don't understand what makes each member of your team tick, it's much harder to plan. Plan for their development, plan for the next project, and plan how to deploy the rich resources of your team to the greatest effect. You can start by asking yourself these questions:

- What do you know about your team members? No, I mean, what do you *really* know about them as individual people?
- Pick one member of the team. What is this person's greatest aspiration?
- What does this person want to do next (e.g., after this role)?
- What are three principles or values that truly guide this person's life?
- How does this person prefer to communicate, both giving and receiving?
- What keeps this person up at night?
- What gets this person out of bed in the morning?
- Why does this person keep coming to work every day to do this job?
- What are three key strengths this person has?

- What talents or skills does this person have that they aren't currently using in this role?
- What has this person gone through to get where they are today?

You could probably quickly jot down some obvious (and superficial) answers to each of those questions. And you're welcome to do that, but you'd be missing the point if you stopped there. If you don't know these things, and more, about every member of your team, you're just a taskmaster.

The better we really know our team members, the more we can improve their quality of life on the team. That result creates deeper trust, which fosters even greater performance. It allows us to really challenge people in ways that would be risky if we hadn't taken the time to understand the person we're pushing. Making assumptions rather than asking better questions leads to loads of missed opportunities.

Big Mike called me about a week after our initial conversation. "Dammit, kid," he boomed over the phone. "Now you've got me thinking."

We ended up working together over a period of two years to get a community center built in his neighborhood. I was there to see the commitments made by the city and other stakeholders, but I had moved on by the time they broke ground and built it. True to his nature, Big Mike saw it through to the end. The center stands serving that community to this day. I recently discovered that Big Mike passed away in 2018, about 20 years after our initial conversations. May he rest in power.

Chapter 5

ASSUMPTIONS AFFECT HOW WE LISTEN

We don't give enough value to fully, actively listening. And we don't need another book about how to do that, we just need someone willing to call us out on the fact that we're not doing it in practice. Someone to tell us to just set the damned phone down, close the laptop, look the other person in the eye, and engage in active listening practices to help us stay focused on what that person is saying to us.

But we don't do any of those things. Why?

Leaders I've worked with have long claimed "too busy" or "managing too many irons in the fire" as excuses. But that's exactly what they are—excuses—and poor ones at that.

The primary reason why we don't stop and fully listen is because of the assumptions that creep in.

We assume we already know what the other person is going to say.

We assume we understand someone else's perspective.

We assume we understand what's motivating, bothering, or upsetting another person.

This failure to truly listen is to our own detriment. By not simply stopping what we're doing and fully listening to the other person, we're wasting so much time. We're missing so much.

I'm sorry. what did you say?

A few years into accepting individual coaching clients—before I went through a year of training to become a certified professional coach—I made a huge mistake. I'd been focused on working with teams, and from that work, every now and then a client would ask me to coach someone one-on-one. At first I had a mild fear of accepting this role. Unfortunately, over time, I had become complacent. No one had died because of my lack of training in this area, so I figured I knew what I was doing.

So what was this huge mistake? I pretended to listen to a client while working on something else.

I know. I can't believe I did that either. Let me tell you what happened.

This was in 2017, and it was a normal workday for me. I had two online coaching sessions on my schedule, plus a call with a previous client who was considering doing another workshop with me. I also had two kids to shuffle off to school, and a farm full of animals to feed and water. My mom was in the early stages of dementia and my parents were living next door at the time. She was often paranoid that I was trying to take control of her life away from her. With her, I never really knew what the day would hold, as my dad was often unable to calm her and would call me for help.

Like I said, it was a pretty normal day.

The kids got off to school, the farm animals got fed and watered, and my wife went to work. Next door, my parents seemed to be having a relatively calm start to their day. I had my first coaching session, and everything was fine. Then came the call with the previous client.

The client wanted to launch a series of workshops in different regions of the country where their offices were clustered. My contact was famous for waiting until the last minute to contract trainers, and this time was no exception. They needed a proposal from me by the end of the day. I was excited about the challenge of creating new workshops for them. My wheels started turning.

There wasn't time before my next coaching session to do more than open my proposal template and fill in the basic info. As the workshops would be custom-designed for this client, I would need to outline them before I could write the content of the proposal.

Going into my next coaching session, I was excited and feeling energized. I was starting to think about how to address the challenges my prospective client wanted me to focus on in the workshops. After that next coaching call, I had a couple of hours free to work on it.

My coaching client was a fairly amiable person in general. He gave lip service to wanting to grow and learn, but he often rejected suggestions of things he could do differently before fully considering or trying them. In addition, his boss was a very difficult person to please. She was a perfectionist and very demanding. My client spent many days feeling like he couldn't win in his interactions with her.

Given these factors, I wasn't surprised when his energy seemed low coming into the session. It didn't send up any red flags because I'd seen him like this before. It was also common for him to want to spend time talking about how things had gone since we last spoke before settling on a topic for that day's discussion. That's how this Zoom session began.

I listened as he started describing the latest interactions he'd had with his boss and colleagues, most of them sounding familiar. I assumed I knew the direction the conversation would go, so I let my wheels go back to turning about the new workshops. I stopped listening to my client, even though I was still nodding and keeping a neutral expression on my face.

Suddenly he stopped talking and was struggling to keep his composure. I realized I had no idea why.

Snapping back to the present moment, I leaned into the screen and waited for him to gather himself and say more. He looked at me expectantly.

I started to sweat. I knew I hadn't been listening. I had assumed the conversation would go along as it always did. I had assumed I knew what he would talk about. But I knew I had missed something here.

"Wait, what?" I asked. My heart was pumping faster than normal, and I was starting to feel a little panicked. "I'm so sorry," I said. "I think I missed something you said."

He stared at me for a moment, looking shocked. "What?"

My face flushed. I felt very embarrassed. "I'm so sorry," I said again. "I missed something you said. I was distracted. Please tell me again."

"I've been let go."

Fuck.

I apologized profusely to my client. I admitted I had been distracted by other things happening in my day and told him there was simply no excuse. I asked for forgiveness and if he would accept my help to plan his next move. We had been working together for nearly six months at that point, so thankfully we had enough of a good foundation built up that he was able to let it go.

I debated long and hard about whether to include this story in this book. I was afraid of damaging my credibility. I was afraid my current coaching clients might read it and always wonder thereafter if I'm really listening to them. I was afraid of your judgment, dear reader.

But this book is about being honest about all the dumb shit we do, even when we know better. It's about coming clean and realizing how extraordinarily common these mistakes are. If I'm not willing to admit to the ugly ways I've done all these things wrong, how can I ask any of you to be honest with yourselves about your own mistakes?

We simply don't listen. In my experience, this is one of the most pervasive ways we make assumptions. We assume that what others are going to say isn't as interesting or important as what's going on in our own heads. We assume these things when, really, we know none of them.

Most of the time there's no malicious intent behind these assumptions. Nor are we actively conscious of or choosing to make them. But that doesn't make the impact any less painful or damaging for those on the receiving end.

It's just an exercise

In 2018, I was contracted to facilitate a workshop with a government agency. As part of the workshop, I did an exercise with the group that was loosely based on the levels of listening identified by Stephen R. Covey in his well-known work *The 7 Habits of Highly Effective People*. After reviewing with them what sort of body language is common with each level of listening, I put them into groups of three.

The first person in each group was the Storyteller. Their job was to think of something interesting that had happened that week to tell the second person. The second person was the Listener. They were to silently choose which level of listening to demonstrate while the story was being told. The third person was the Observer. Their job was to watch the interaction and try to guess which level of listening was being displayed.

This is a fast-paced exercise and often gets quite animated. In nearly every group I've ever done it with, a significant portion of the room uses this simulation to do what they'd never consciously do in real life—be a terrible listener. There's often a lot of laughter as people blatantly display their lack of listening.

Watching the management group as they began, I anticipated a similar experience. Throughout most of the room, the exercise was unfolding as it usually did, with some people overtly listening and some people overtly not listening. There were chuckles and the typical responses. I called time on the first round and asked the Observers to make their guesses. Once they did, I asked the Listeners to confirm or deny the accuracy of the guesses.

We went on to the second round. In every group, the roles rotated one person to the left. I glanced over at the group off to one side, and something about the way one member of the group had his arms crossed over his chest caused me to sense tension. I watched that group as they got started on the second round. There were no smiles.

As soon as the Storyteller spoke his first words, the Listener, the man who had had his arms folded, picked his phone up off the table, turned on his heel, and walked across the room. I had seen that before, and the group usually had a laugh about it. This group wasn't laughing. The Storyteller and Observer looked a little uneasy, and the Listener just looked mad as he walked away.

Time was up for round two, so anyone who had chosen to walk away from their group to display a total lack of listening returned to their group. As we repeated the exercise of guessing and affirming, I was still watching that one group out of the corner of my eye. I told everyone that for this final round, as they rotated roles one last time, the Listener should model how they'd like to be treated when speaking.

The group I'd been watching seemed to comply as the new Storyteller and new Listener began to interact. The angry guy was now the Observer and still standing with his arms crossed. The other two still seemed a little uneasy but were focusing more on each other than on him.

When the exercise ended, I asked everyone to have a seat. I tried to keep things light by telling them I was about to ask a "how did that feel" question while also promising the session wouldn't turn "touchy-feely." That got some chuckles.

I asked, "In all seriousness, how many of you had the experience of your Listener modeling something other than the highest levels of listening?" About three-quarters of the room raised their hands. I nodded. "Very common," I said. "Why did those of you who chose to model less than the highest levels of listening choose to do so?"

There were a few comments around the room about how it was kind of amusing to use an exercise like this to demonstrate what they didn't like done to them.

"And how did that feel?" I asked, smiling at them. The Listeners responded that it felt a little mean and disrespectful, but also a little like they were getting away with something they'd never consciously do in real life.

Then I asked the Storytellers how it felt to have that done to them. There was again agreement around the room that it hadn't felt very nice.

I kept glancing at the angry guy who was sitting, arms still folded, but leaning on the table now. When I caught his eye, I asked, "Can I ask you what you were feeling during the exercise when you were being the Storyteller?"

He stared at me for a moment and then said, "Pissed off." No one laughed. Everyone had picked up on the tension. "Will you share why?" I asked gently.

He launched into a mini tirade about how his Listener hadn't listened at all and how it had instantly infuriated him. He talked about how this same dynamic happened way too often in the office between colleagues and that it felt like a slap in the face.

Most workshops in which I've used this exercise don't elicit a reaction this strong, but there's definitely a level of irritation from people who feel they aren't being heard during the activity. This man made the connection between how shitty it felt to be ignored in a simulated exercise and how it feels in real life. After further discussion, the managers agreed that they wanted to collectively strive to listen better. While the angry guy relaxed some as the discussion went on, the exercise had clearly touched a nerve.

This happens in many workplaces. I hear from teams often about it. Every group seems to have one or two people who are notorious for "listening" while actually focusing on their phones or laptops. The pull to keep working and be "productive" fools us into thinking we're multitasking when, in reality, there's no such thing. Our brains can't do two tasks at the same time. Some of us are hardwired to be able to switch tasks very quickly, which makes us feel like we're multitasking, but we really aren't.

When we're trying to listen to someone and do something else at the same time, we're not able to fully listen.

We're also not able to give our full attention to the other thing we've been trying to do, so it's a lose–lose proposition. The person we're half-listening to knows it and feels it. Those feelings range from mild irritation to fury. This experience can erode the trust in the relationship. It can make the other person less likely to approach us or ask us for support. It can cause us to lose their respect.

Listening for the wrong reasons

When I was growing up, my parents didn't spend a lot of time with their families. My mom's family all moved out to Colorado and Arizona when I was little, and my dad's family wasn't close with us. Neighbors and friends became chosen family. It was rare to have a night at the family dinner table that didn't include at least one other person outside of our core family of four.

One woman in particular was a close friend of my parents and came to dinner nearly every night while I was in high school. She and I butted heads sometimes, as we were both strong-willed. She had been raised very differently from how my mom was raising me, and she often felt entitled to step in and try to parent me. I resisted. I didn't trust her.

One of the reasons I didn't trust her was because of how she "listened" to people, including me. She was a teacher and a department head at a prominent Detroit magnet high school, the chief rival of the one I attended. She was used to commanding a room and being the voice of expertise. That expectation seemed to carry over into all her relationships.

This woman was full of assumptions about what my mother would say next or what my father was asking for on the table. But the worst was whenever I told a story to my parents about something that had happened that day at school. I knew she was listening because of all the comments she would interject, but she wasn't listening to understand. She wasn't focused on hearing my perspective. She was listening in order to top me.

For every story I told, this woman seemed to have a story about something just a little bit "more"—a little bit worse, a little bit better, a little bit scarier or more upsetting, a little bit funnier, you name it. It got so that I would tell a story just to see if she could top me. She always did.

Many years later, Saturday Night Live had a skit about a character named Penelope, played by Kristen Wiig, who did this exact thing during traffic school.[2] When I saw it, I laughed out loud and yelled, "That's my mom's friend!" At the time I was living through it, however, it wasn't funny to me at all. It was infuriating.

This woman's approach had the effect of completely eroding my respect for her. I didn't like her by the time I graduated and went off to college. Every kid just wants their parent (or parent figure) to listen to them. She took over the room so much that my mother, who wasn't a

---

[2] Saturday Night Live, "Penelope: Traffic School—SNL," YouTube, September 20, 2013, video, 4:58, https://www.youtube.com/watch?v=NCjjx8A-jfE.

wallflower by any stretch, just sat back. When I protested to my mother, she defended her friend, telling me not to be disrespectful. It was damaging to our relationship as well.

Listening isn't an all-or-nothing proposition. There are many shades of gray. The levels of listening we talked about in that workshop exercise were rooted in Stephen Covey's work, as I mentioned before. The levels start at the bottom with Ignoring (Level One) and move up to Empathetic (Level Five). Here they are outlined briefly:[3]

- Level One: Ignoring—This level may seem like the worst one. Who wants to be completely ignored? Wasn't that exactly what got the guy in the first story so upset? The reason I argue that it's not actually the worst level is because the signs are usually pretty clear. If someone on a video call is on mute, typing away and not looking at the screen, it's obvious that they aren't listening. While infuriating, at least it's clear.

- Level Two: Pretending—This happens when we try to appear as though we're listening but really aren't. In fact, I've noticed people will often say, "I'm listening" as they look away at their computer screen or phone or watch what someone else is doing. People who are pretending to listen miss things in more obvious ways. They might be looking at you, or even nodding along with what you're saying. They aren't actually listening, but they are actively trying to give you the impression that they are.

---

[3] Stephen R. Covey, *The 7 Habits of Highly Effective People: Powerful Lessons in Personal Change* (New York: Free Press, 2004).

This was the level at which I was operating with my client when I missed him telling me that he'd been let go.

- Level Three: Selective—This happens when we listen only for our next opportunity to speak. We don't necessarily interrupt, but we're listening for our chance to tell *our* story, give *our* example, or prove something. This is exactly what happened to me in the first story I shared in chapter 1. While sitting at the table with the group from Antioch Baptist Church, my only reason for "listening" was to find my opportunity to prove I belonged there. It's also what happened on a daily basis with my mom's friend. She listened only for her opportunity to tell me and everyone else how much "more" her own experience was.

- Level Four: Attentive—Many people think this is the ultimate level of listening. Better conversations happen at this level because people are actively listening to one another's words. But at this level we're still operating from our own desire to be understood. We're still busy formulating what we want to say next while listening to the other person. This level is still transactional.

- Level Five: Empathetic—The paradigm shifts deeply when we get to this level. Our own agenda disappears, and it becomes all about the other person. We are driven to keep asking questions, probe deeper, and reserve judgment about what's being said by the other person. We are seeking to understand the other person before seeking to be understood, as Covey describes. This level is where magic happens in conversations or meetings.

Pretending to listen and selective listening are the worst levels of listening. Someone operating at one of those levels knows they should be listening but has decided not to give someone their full attention. That decision may be subconscious, but it's still a decision. Common assumptions baked into this behavior are that they already know what someone is going to say or that what someone has to say won't interest them enough to give that person their full attention. With some trepidation, I've already admitted in this book to several examples of doing exactly this. And there are more coming.

I could take the attitude of shame with this behavior. But in exercising that kind of judgment about my behavior, I miss the opportunity to fully examine it and ultimately learn from it. Sharing my honest foibles and reflections on them with you is an invitation for you to do the same. It's only through reflecting and digesting our experiences that we create an opportunity to do better.

And in the meantime, we've all had many moments of getting it right, even if it's by accident. Meet Maria.

An example of not guessing your way through it

I met Maria when she became my housekeeper in Nicaragua. I had resisted, to the point of exhaustion, the idea of having a housekeeper. When I finally gave in and hired Maria upon the recommendation of our neighbor, I couldn't believe I had waited so long. Life in rural Nicaragua was hard, and managing a household while working full time was simply impossible. (Clearly, my need to justify and explain it here indicates my ongoing discomfort with the situation, but I digress.)

I had been warned by someone I felt I could trust that housekeepers were dishonest. She thought it was important to be inherently suspicious of them as a group. Classism was alive and well in that community.

When Maria had been with us for almost a month and it had been going really well, I decided to work from home one morning until I had to leave for a meeting out in one of the villages. Maria didn't know I was at home that morning. I had no reason to distrust her but found myself watching the clock as I cleaned up my breakfast dishes to see what time she would come by. We had agreed she would start at 8:30 or 9:00 a.m. each morning.

Near 10:00 a.m., her eldest daughter, Meylin, came to the front door, which had a metal security gate instead of a screen door like I was accustomed to back home in Michigan. She was a little breathless and looked nervous. I wiped my hands on a towel as I walked into the front room, beginning to feel a little alarmed.

"Good morning, Doña Elena," she said, catching her breath. "I looked for you in your office, but they told me you were at home this morning, so I ran over here."

I reached the front door gate and unlocked it as I said, "That's okay, honey, come on in. Where is your mom? Is everything okay?"

Meylin stepped into the house, her glance darting around at everything, including up at my face. "My mother is not able to come today, so she sent me in her place to do her job for her. She is hoping to be able to return tomorrow. What would you like me to do first?"

"Wait, wait, hold on," I said, holding my hand up. "Is your mom okay? Is she sick?" I was feeling less alarmed and a little more irritated now. I immediately assumed my friend had been right about housekeepers. With the rest of the conversation already playing out in my head, I was sure I knew the direction this was going.

Meylin wouldn't look me in the eye. "She's just not able to come today," she repeated. She sounded like she was carefully reciting only what she had been instructed to say, no more.

I decided not to push her. "Well," I said, "I actually am on my way out to a village in a little while, so go ahead and go back home. Let your mother know that she should come back as soon as she's able and that if there is anything I can do, she should let me know."

Meylin was reluctant to go. "But my mother sent me here to do her work! She will not be happy with me if I go home without doing it."

"Okay," I said, turning and walking back into the kitchen. "I'll write her a note that you can take to her, explaining everything." I took a piece of paper from my small notebook and began writing a note. I chose my words carefully so as not to get Meylin in trouble or offend Maria.

The girl was still reluctant to go, but she finally took the note and let herself out of the front gate. Once she had carefully closed it behind her, she trotted off down the street, note in hand.

Later that evening when I came back from work, I found Maria waiting at my kitchen table. As soon as I saw her, I knew my assumption had been wrong and felt embarrassed. She was sitting watching the door, her hands clasped tightly on the table in front of her. Her face was drawn and her jaw was set tightly. Something was wrong.

As I approached her, she interpreted my embarrassment as being upset with her. She jumped up from the table and immediately began apologizing for startling me and showing up unannounced.

I sat down at the table with her and motioned for her to sit again as well. I shook my head, saying, "No, Maria, I was just worried about you. It didn't seem that you were simply not feeling well; it seemed as though something might be wrong."

Maria wrung her hands together, her dark eyes darting around as if she wasn't sure where to focus. She was visibly nervous and looked as though she was trying to decide how much to trust me.

"Maria, if you're in some kind of trouble, please tell me so that I can help you." I reached across the table and gently touched her hands. She jumped a little. I quickly withdrew my hand and said, "I'm sorry."

"No, no, Doña Elena, it is me that is sorry. I did not mean to make you worry, and I am sorry that I am so nervous right now." She craned her neck to look out into the front room. "Did you lock the gate? It's after dark now."

Now I knew my assumption had been way off base, and I was starting to feel scared. I got up to check the front door gate. It was locked. I came back to the kitchen table, saying, "Okay, Maria, now you're starting to scare me. What's going on? Please tell me."

After a pause and a deep breath, she said, "Doña Elena, I was with the father of my two younger children for 10 years. Meylin is not his child; she was born before I knew him. My ex is not a nice man. After a lot of abuse, we separated. Every now and then, he comes back. He is not welcome in our home, so he gets very angry and sometimes violent when I tell him to go away. A couple of days after I started working for you, he came to my house late at night. We were all in bed sleeping, and the house was locked up tight. He started pounding and yelling—he was drunk—and when we wouldn't open the door, he broke it down."

She paused, her breathing a little heavier, her fear palpable. Cold fear was gripping me as well.

"Oh my God, Maria," I breathed out, completely drawn into her story and unable to imagine what might've happened next. "What happened? Are you and the kids okay?"

She nodded. "My neighbors heard what was happening and came to tell him to leave. He was so drunk that after using his energy to break down my door, he didn't have any left to harm us, so he left. The reason I couldn't come to work today is because I filed for a restraining order against him and today was the court date. I had to go to court to explain why I need this restraining order. I had to wait there most of the day. I just got done a couple of hours ago, and then I came here."

She paused, clearly struggling to go on. "I had to wait most of the day," she repeated. She looked up at me finally, her shame and pain written all over her features. "And he was right there, on the next bench, also waiting." She was whispering now, trying to hold her chin up and her tears back at the same time. I was having trouble holding back my own.

I've had too many experiences and heard too many stories of women not being believed for one reason or another when they were victims of some type of violence or abuse. I took a breath to calm myself. I didn't want to make Maria think I was upset with her.

"Maria, I respect your decision to do what you felt was going to keep you safe. I hope that you know now that I trust you and do believe you. Thank you for trusting me enough to share the truth about today and that night with me."

I ducked my head to try to catch her eyes, which were focused down at her hands as if she was awaiting a verdict. When she finally looked up at me, I said again, "Thank you for trusting me. Is there anything you need?"

She smiled and finally relaxed a little bit. "No, thank you. I should probably get home to my kids now. They are at my sister's house. I was afraid to leave them home alone."

"Maria, is the door fixed? Do you need a new door?"

She smiled again, a little sadly, and rose from the table. "No, thank you, Doña Elena. We are just fine. Enjoy your evening now. I'll see you tomorrow. Good night."

I walked her to the front gate and unlocked it to let her out into the twilight. She closed it behind her with the same gentle care that I had seen in Meylin earlier in the day. She gave me a quick smile and started to walk away.

Suddenly she turned and said quietly, "Doña Elena, be sure you lock that gate." I nodded and then quickly turned the key as she stood watching to make sure I did it.

I'm not sure whether it was the gripping nature of Maria's story that made it impossible to do anything except listen with rapt attention or my embarrassment over realizing my initial assumptions about her had been so far off base. But there was no option for listening at any other level than completely in that moment that evening. As Maria shared her story with me, I couldn't even guess where things would go next.

I've had many of my own #MeToo experiences in my life, including several that year I was in Nicaragua. When we hear stories to which we can relate, it's natural to want to share our own as well. But empathetically listening to another person and creating space for them to tell their story is a sacred act. When we put our own need to be heard on the back burner to be fully present for someone else, it's powerful. And that doesn't have to be just for stories like Maria's.

Stop what you're doing. Put down your phone. Look the person you need to listen to in the eye. Suspend all assumptions or judgments about what you think they're going to say. It can be a powerful act, particularly when you hear a story like Maria's. But it's an equally important way to respond to someone who's just asking for your help on a project.

Chapter 6

ASSUMPTIONS AFFECT HOW (AND IF) WE BUILD TRUST

Y ou're in the thick of it. You've got workplace relationships that aren't going as well as you'd like. You wonder, "How can I shift boats mid-stream to change to
a better outcome?"

One way to make such a course correction is by assessing
and recognizing when and how we're making assumptions
about our colleagues. Those assumptions can be a substan-
tial barrier between us, making it difficult to build trust.

Building trust is foundational to productive relationships with people in our workplace. Taking the time out
of our regular daily grind to ask someone to share their
stories with us helps us abandon the assumptions we may
have been making about them. We get to see them with

fresh eyes, seeking to understand rather than just assuming we already know who and how they are.

When I listen to someone tell their stories, they tell me they feel seen and heard. As the listener, I feel humbled that they are willing to be open with me. This is a very powerful way to cultivate trust, loyalty, connection, and feeling valued. Those feelings on both sides make it exponentially easier to ask questions during the normal routine of daily work life. As a result, we all make far fewer unproductive assumptions.

Building trust intentionally is not unprofessional. In fact, I would argue it's one of the most respectful things we can do.

Simple. Maybe not always easy, but definitely simple.

In my early years as a community organizer in the late '90s, I worked in Northwest Indiana. The churches in my territory were based in East Chicago and Hammond, near Gary. After a few experiences like the one I described in chapter 1 with Antioch Baptist Church, I realized my assumptions about the people I encountered were preventing me from building trust with them.

Pastor Blakely, the pastor of one of the churches in my group, had been working with my organization for a little while but hadn't really gotten his congregation involved yet. One day I asked Pastor Blakely if we could sit down to talk. I had some guesses (assumptions) about why he was holding back on getting his congregation involved, and I wanted to test them out.

Our previous conversations had always been very respectful and cordial, but also very superficial. I was a 25-year-old white girl from Detroit, and he was a Black man in his late 50s from the South. I suspected one of the challenges of going deeper in the conversation came from a fundamental lack of trust on both sides.

I started by asking his permission to get to know him better and telling him I wished to deepen my understanding of his congregation and gain his perspective on issues of importance facing the community. He agreed, and I began by inviting him to tell me about how he grew up.

As the conversation progressed, I let my curiosity about his life lead me. I listened to his stories and asked follow-up questions to help me understand how his experiences had influenced his current perspectives. I offered information about myself only if he talked about an experience or a place with which I was familiar. Even then I restricted my comments to letting him know I was familiar with what he was describing, but I always brought the conversation right back to him.

Eventually I asked what his vision was for his congregation. After he shared with me the broader vision every pastor has of growing, serving, and being a light in the community, I asked him how he felt his involvement in my organization might support this vision. He hesitated. I could almost feel the barrier we'd just bumped up against.

I decided to test my assumptions. I told Pastor Blakely I had sensed some hesitance on his part to get his congregation involved and asked him if that was true. He agreed that it was, and I asked if he could help me understand why.

He hesitated again. I waited quietly. After a few moments, he began to explain that trust issues caused him to feel protective of his congregation and reluctant to get them involved.

Taking a deep breath and gathering my courage, I asked him if he was sure he knew that's what they wanted. He stared at me for a moment, and I was afraid he would ask me to leave. I started to explain that I meant absolutely no disrespect in asking the question, but he shook his head. I started to apologize, and he held up his hand. Then he said softly, "I don't."

I waited.

"I don't know if that's what they want," he continued. "I haven't asked."

I matched his soft tone and body language, and we continued to discuss why that was and what he wanted to do about it. He agreed I should meet a few of his key leaders and build relationships with them as a starting point to possibly inviting their involvement.

That conversation was a turning point in our relationship. Everything shifted after that because we had built a foundation of trust that went beyond the superficial. Every time I saw Pastor Blakely at another event from then on, he would nod if we weren't close enough to speak and greet me warmly if we were.

He also introduced me to his key leaders, and I began building relationships with them, taking the same approach I'd taken with him. I learned that they were all frustrated with the lack of younger people showing interest in leadership. When I asked them why they thought that was, they all assumed they already knew why. They assumed it was that the younger people didn't really care. They assumed that it was because the younger people were just too busy. They all said some version of the same thing, which was that the younger people simply didn't care as much as they did.

I asked all of them where those beliefs (assumptions) were coming from. Had they had conversations with the young people about this? No. They "just knew." I thanked them for sharing their insights with me and left it there.

When I regrouped with Pastor Blakely after this meeting with his key leaders, I shared the conclusion (assumption) his key leaders had come to about the young people. He laughed and confessed that he shared that belief (assumption) but recognized he wasn't sure it was true. He said he wanted to invite his congregation to take a closer look.

Subsequently I worked with him to organize what we dubbed a "Listening Campaign" in his church. I trained a group of leaders and members who were interested in conducting these one-on-one relationship-building conversations with a cross section of the church membership. The campaign went on for about eight weeks, and the group of "listeners" talked with about a third of the congregation.

When we came together to debrief, some of the key leaders looked defensive. A couple of them looked sheepish. When the group started sharing the general feedback from the one-on-one conversations, it became clear that some younger people had in fact made multiple attempts to join the leadership team. In most cases, they had felt their new ideas weren't welcomed by the "old guard." One gentleman from that "old guard" commented loudly to his neighbor, "Maybe that's because their ideas weren't any good."

I could've let the comment go by, but a few people murmured in response, and I sensed they didn't agree with it. I also thought it was probably not true. I turned to the man who had made the comment and politely asked him if he would mind sharing his perspective with the group, as I thought there might be something important to discuss in what he had said.

He did so, and a productive discussion ensued. With some encouragement, they identified a few concrete action steps they wanted to take to increase involvement, especially by the young people. Also, after discovering that a core group was interested in one of the issue campaigns my organization was working on, they decided to invite people to participate in that as well.

The assumptions Pastor Blakely and I had made about each other had initially prevented us from building trust. The assumptions Pastor Blakely had made about his congregation and their interest in being involved had kept him from creating opportunities for them to grow along with the organization. The assumptions the key leaders in his congregation had made about why more people weren't stepping up to help out had prevented them from building trust with those people, and it had prevented them from growing their leadership base.

When we realize we've been operating with assumptions, we can consciously choose to step back and test them out. I've used this technique for building trust through one-on-one conversations with many corporate clients. The teams I've worked with to show them how to have these conversations and then given a chance to try it out with each other have been surprised by the results. I've had leaders come back from their one-on-one conversations realizing they didn't know much at all about their one-on-one partner. Other leaders have reported being surprised at how much they learned about their one-on-one partner, even though they'd worked together for years.

There's something about carving out intentional space to invite someone to tell you their story with no other agenda. We all want to be seen and heard, and this is one simple, if not always easy way we can do that for each other.

Mind the (generation) gaps

If you've ever been to London and ridden the subway, you've heard the announcer say, "Mind the gap" as you step onto or off the train cars. It's a phrase that has stuck with me ever since 1993 when I was studying abroad in Paris for a semester and visited London for the first time with my parents. Whenever I hear people talk about generation gaps, this phrase comes back to me and I hear "Mind the generation gap" in my head. Silly, I know.

In 2018, I led a series of workshops for a client, duplicating the workshop experience in each of the five regions where the client had teams of store managers. At the end of each workshop, I asked the group to identify what they wanted to work on next. What were the biggest communication challenges they faced in their stores with staff? The universal response? Generation gaps. I probed a little bit to better understand what specifically they felt challenged by. A large Gen X representation in the group expressed frustration with millennials. A number of baby boomers in the group said they found both the millennials and the Gen Xers frustrating. And the few millennials in the group sat with their arms folded, their body language signaling that they felt attacked. I asked them to weigh in, and they said they simply didn't feel like either generation wanted to listen to them.

I designed the next series of workshops for 2019, and the issue of generation differences was first on the agenda. Depending on how you slice them up, there are five generations represented in the workplace at any given time. Each generation has a stereotypical communication style. Of course there are exceptions to every rule, but the older you are, the stronger your preference will likely be for hierarchy and traditional, more formal ways. The younger you are, the stronger your preference will likely be for flexibility in all areas, including communication.

I let the group get nice and entrenched in their assumptions about each generation different from their own. I showed them how to do one-on-ones, the intentional trust-building conversation. Then I paired them up, crossing generations within each pair, and told them to get to know each other better.

They came back about an hour later, and we debriefed. They observed how much more they had in common with their partner than they had originally thought they would. Without exception, they expressed surprise and delight with what they had learned about each other. It didn't take much to get them to come to the conclusion that generation gaps are largely built on assumptions we project onto someone of a different age. They also concluded that such assumptions can be easily overcome simply by building trust through getting to know one another better.

When in doubt, ask

The Socratic method of asking questions for the purpose of finding truth has long held up as a gold standard in many arenas. However, somewhere along the way, asking questions to clarify understanding seems to have become shunned.

The junior member of a team is eager to please and do a good job, for example. While receiving his instructions from his team lead, he thinks he understands what to do but isn't completely certain. The team lead simply gives him a double thumbs-up and says, "You good to go?" while starting to back away from the meeting. The junior member hesitates, wondering whether he should just double-check his understanding. But he assumes the team lead will think he's dumb or slow to learn if he does, so he gives a thumbs-up back and says, "Yes!"

Back at his desk, he doesn't know where to start. Now what?

We've done a great job of creating a culture in which asking questions implies we lack intelligence. Somewhere between high school and college, I remember getting the distinct impression that the only questions that were "allowed" were ones that built on the concept being discussed. Questions to clarify understanding of the concept itself indicated you weren't keeping up. Recently, I spoke to a group of college summer interns and asked if this was also their experience. They all confirmed that it was.

I'd like to officially object.

If the team lead had been doing a great job managing his new team member, this whole scenario would've gone differently from the beginning. The team lead would have stopped at each step of the process to confirm the junior member's understanding and encourage questions about how to implement the instructions. He might've even shown the junior member where to go to get started. He definitely would've made sure the junior member knew he shouldn't hesitate to come back with any question at all, no matter how small or silly it might seem.

But that didn't happen. Let's go back to what our junior team member is now experiencing. He's at his desk and realizes he doesn't know where to start. He's embarrassed about not remembering or understanding everything, and he doesn't want to look bad in front of his new boss. Now what?

By not asking for help or clarification at the outset, he's potentially going to make mistakes. If that happens, he could create more problems for himself, for the team, or for the project.

Despite any discomfort or embarrassment, he should ask. He could approach the team lead and explain, "As this is a new project/process for me, I want to double-check my understanding of how to get started. I got back to my desk and realized it wasn't as clear to me as I thought. Would you mind going over the first step again with me?" But way too often, this doesn't happen. The junior team member may instead wring his hands, try to figure it out on his own, or wait for a clue from someone else.

From what our clients tell us, this kind of thing happens frequently in businesses of all kinds. People are convinced that their assumptions are true and that they will lose face or credibility from asking questions. This blocks them from asking for help, showing any vulnerability, and, ultimately, from building relationships in the workplace based on trust. But why?

Our clients tell us that it's fear stopping them—fear of looking scattered or unprepared, fear of looking "dumb," fear of being deemed "lacking" in a performance review. When challenged about this thinking, most of them eventually realize asking for help or clarification isn't a weakness. But there are a few who remain adamant in their conviction that asking questions equates to some sort of deficiency on their part. They steadfastly refuse to ask those clarifying kinds of questions. What a shame.

If that's really the kind of workplace you're in, why would you stay in such a toxic environment? If there's no room for questions to clarify understanding, what does that say about the culture? What does it say about your boss?

An example of not guessing your way through it

In 1999, Friendship Baptist Church in Northwest Indiana got a new pastor. He was a very shy, quiet man, unlike his predecessor and many of his colleagues. He didn't command the room. He'd received his calling later in life after 20 years working in the steel mills and didn't radiate confidence as a pastor.

The church he pastored was one in my territory, but I hadn't met very many people from the church. The previous pastor had been an older gentleman who had been in ill health for a time before passing, and aside from participating in small numbers at organization-wide events, the church wasn't very active in the organization.

I was curious about the new pastor, so I invited him to meet with me so I could get to know him. He agreed. I was a little surprised and a lot delighted at how willing he seemed to be to tell me his story. I realized while listening to him that I'd been assuming he would be closed off and difficult to draw out, given how shy he seemed in public.

I was 26 at the time, so clearly I lacked the maturity to see how much I didn't know yet about the world. I remember thinking how much more there was to him than I had expected. I cringe at the arrogance of that thought now, but I was oblivious to it at the time.

Thankfully, my training as an organizer helped me keep asking questions to learn more, understand his perspective and experiences, and listen deeply. What I heard was a man who knew how the world saw him: shy, quiet, always smiling, and easygoing. He described situations when he'd been walked on because of those traits and frustration at not being taken seriously. I started seeing possibilities.

Over the course of a few weeks, the pastor allowed me to conduct one-on-ones with the key group of leaders in the church. He didn't yet have deep relationships with many of them, so I was surprised that he allowed me to have access to them. He seemed to see me as someone who could help him in his journey to success, and I was so honored by that. I really didn't want to mess it up.

As I met people in the church, I heard stories about life in that community that were troubling. There's heavy train traffic running through Northwest Indiana, and two sets of tracks ran through the community where this church sat and into southern Chicago. Train companies were fined for stopping on the tracks and blocking road crossings for any length of time. The fines were significantly higher in Illinois than they were in Indiana. It was very common to wait for more than 30 minutes for a train to move in northwest Indiana, just outside of Chicago and the Illinois border. In some areas, like where this church sat, there was no way around the tracks.

There were also drug dealers in the neighborhood and occasional gun violence. One Sunday, as church was letting out, a van came careening into the parking lot, nearly hitting several churchgoers. The man driving had been shot in a nearby incident and had passed out while trying to drive away. Someone called 911 immediately, but trains were sitting parked on the nearby tracks, waiting for traffic in Illinois to clear. The ambulance couldn't get through, and the man died.

I heard more stories of gun violence in that neighborhood as well. One member of the church, an older woman, had been sitting on her couch watching TV one evening when a drive-by shooting happened a block over. A stray bullet came through her wall, and she was hit. No ambulance could reach her in time either.

I heard these stories only because I opened up conversations with members of the church who lived in the community. I made no assumptions regarding what they cared about. I didn't go in with an agenda to get them involved in the metropolitan issues my organization was working on. Instead, I went in and listened. I invited them to tell me what mattered to them and what they saw happening around them. From there, I invited them to do something about it. They organized and carried out a series of local actions, and before long, there was an ambulance permanently stationed at the fire station in their neighborhood.

Time spent building trust with people in our workplaces is never time wasted. The more we trust each other, the easier everything gets.

You can find tons of things written about generation gaps and the general lack of trust in the workplace today. I'm not here to duplicate those ideas. My area of interest is in what we do with those gaps and lack of trust. How do people communicate effectively? Build trust? Cross the generation gap? Close it? Here are a few ideas to consider.

Think back to when you entered the workforce. How did older workers respond to you? What helped you? What hindered you? When you interact with colleagues from other generations, what barriers do you find? What do you have in common?

Let's extend it beyond generational differences. Think about the people you work with on a regular basis. Before you approach someone, think about what you've noticed about them. How do they seem to prefer to interact with other people? If they've reached out to you before, have they done so through email? By phone? Through an app of some sort?

If you don't really know much about someone's preferences for communicating, you might try asking questions like the following:

- Do you have a preferred way to communicate about projects?
- How would you like me to keep you updated? How often? By what method?
- What's the best way to get feedback from you? How about to give feedback?
- If I have a quick question about something, what's the best way to ask you (call, text, message, etc.)?

In addition to these very specific questions, you can get a lot out of a working relationship when you show interest in the other person by asking the following kinds of questions:

- How did you get your start in the industry?
- What attracted you to your career choice?
- Where did you grow up?
- What was that like?
- Who are your heroes?
- What do you value in a coworker?
- What's the last book you read?

Questions that show genuine interest in who somebody is, what they care about, and how they like to work are very effective for building trust. The more trust you build, the less likely you are to make assumptions about another person. At the very least, trust can lower the barriers to asking clarifying questions.

Chapter 7

ASSUMPTIONS AFFECT OUR ABILITY TO SET BOUNDARIES

When we have inappropriate expectations about what we can (and should) be getting from a professional working relationship, it becomes difficult to create healthy boundaries in that relationship. We can create healthy boundaries in both our public and private lives by drawing lines between the two spheres. And we can draw those lines by differentiating the expectations we have with each set of relationships.

As I said way back in the introduction, unmet expectations are almost always the result of assumptions. For example, we expect everyone to like us at work. When we don't have a "friendly" relationship with someone we work with, our response to that person stems directly from our assumptions about the expectation that they should like us. Our actions will be informed by this assumption. We may start leaving them off email chains they really should be part of or avoiding being in the break room at the same time as them. We may begin to take it personally that they don't seem to like us.

But why is that the goal at work?

While having coworkers like us might be one of the nice side effects of working together, it's dangerous to focus on such an outcome as a goal. It keeps us from making difficult decisions and, sometimes, from doing what's right.

Blurring the lines

In 2020, when I began working on a different book (prior to this one) and was looking for an editor, a book coach I'd been working with recommended one. My book coach hadn't been collaborating with this editor for very long, but she had an excellent reputation in the publishing world, and his initial contacts with her seemed to live up to those expectations. I decided to have an initial call with the editor to explore the process.

Her credentials were impressive, the list of names of people she had worked with was star-studded, and her manner was eccentric but charming. She was full of praise for the writing sample I'd sent her. I was hooked.

Our initial conversations and communications showed respect for the boundaries of my private life. If she proposed a consultation outside of normal business hours, she always checked to make sure it wouldn't interfere with my family life.

That book was a memoir, based on the year I had spent in Nicaragua. I'd released it initially several years ago as a completely self-published piece and had never felt comfortable marketing it alongside my coaching and consulting business because the story is deeply personal. Yet I know it resonates with clients because I've told pieces of it in workshops for years. I wanted to find a way to rework it and rerelease it.

My editor could see herself in the pages of my story. She'd had experiences that were similar in nature and began sharing some of her experiences with me during our consultations. At first it helped strengthen the trust and rapport we were building as two professional women working together. She shared things about her current living situation that she felt were experiences I could relate to. She was a woman alone in a small town trying to get contractors and other help to restore an old farmhouse. With every experience she was having, however, she seemed to be projecting herself more and more into my story, and I started to feel mildly uncomfortable.

In spite of that, I felt her editing feedback was gold. I was getting the kind of clarity about that story I felt I'd missed before. I also became clear on where that story belonged, and it wasn't in my business. I decided to shelve that project and began working on this book instead. We took a break from working together while I did some initial writing.

During the first few months I was working with her, the editor had become more relaxed in how she talked to me. She had begun using terms of endearment with me. At first they felt maternal and seemed appropriate, given the nature of the story I was sharing. Until they didn't.

I have a habit of replying to emails when I have time, rather than making sure the replies are being delivered during normal business hours. I'd never considered it to be a problem before. In this case, it seemed to signal to my editor that I was available at all hours.

That November, I was traveling for a client and got to my hotel room on a Sunday afternoon. I hadn't caught up on email for a couple of days and would be engaged in a workshop for the coming two days, so I decided to sit down and take care of it then. One of the messages was from my editor. I had let her know that I felt the new book was at a place where I was ready to resume working together, and her message confirmed she was ready to move forward. I replied, indicating my enthusiasm to get working again.

About five minutes after I hit send, I got a text message from her asking if I was free to talk for a few minutes, saying it was somewhat urgent. Since I knew I wouldn't be able to speak with her for a couple of days, I replied that I was free.

That conversation was the first colossal red flag. She poured her heart out to me about all the challenges she was facing: first an ailing relative who had no one but her to turn to for help and how she'd saved his life the day before; then a tree that had fallen and done damage to her house, and how she was having a terrible time getting anyone to come fix it; then her car that had broken down, and how the man sent by the towing company to get it was acting suspiciously, so she'd sent him away and was now stranded.

I listened to her, told her I was sorry to hear all that she was going through, and asked if it would be better for us to resume working together when she was more settled. She told me she didn't have anyone else to talk to because she'd recently lost all her phone contacts through another mishap and both of her closest friends were going through major life events and couldn't be there for her. She said that working with me on this project was a lifeline for her.

I should've politely extracted myself from the conversation and disengaged at that point. But I didn't. I had hyped this woman's ability to help me as an editor so much in my mind that I couldn't yet see where this would go. I thought she was just having a rough week. (Naïve, I know. Thanks, hindsight.)

I didn't tell anyone about the conversation. I soon became aware that I wasn't telling anyone about that conversation or any other uncomfortable things I'd noticed during my interactions with this editor. The not telling was another red flag for me, but I continued to ignore it.

In the two weeks that followed, the conversations just got weirder. None of it was about my work, even though I had paid for the next round of editing. She made many references to outside forces trying to harm or sabotage her and was convinced some of what was happening was retribution for experiences she'd had overseas in the recent past.

These were the experiences she felt were similar in nature to mine in Nicaragua. I wasn't sure they were all that similar, but that didn't seem to matter to her.

The final straw was a phone call just before Thanksgiving. She was noticeably agitated and paranoid, and I had trouble following all the ins and outs of her story. She was calling from someone else's phone, and they came to get the phone back before she was ready to end the call. I listened to her argue with this man before she came back on the line with me and pleaded with me to contact the FBI.

I was speechless. And knew I needed some help at that point. I called my best friend and told her everything. She has a lot of experience with mental illness in people very close to her, so I was sure she'd be able to help me understand what I should do. She confirmed that it sounded like my editor might be experiencing a mental health episode of some sort.

I called the hotel where my editor had told me she was staying, and I spoke with the manager. She agreed that my editor seemed "not herself," as she had stayed at this small inn before during renovations on her farmhouse. She said my editor had left abruptly but that the staff already had a plan to call for a mental health check with local authorities if she returned.

I spent that Thanksgiving weekend with my stomach in knots. The signs I had chosen to ignore became obvious after I talked to other people about what I'd been experiencing with this woman. All kinds of lines between our public and private lives had been crossed. And I had participated just as much as she had by allowing it to go unchecked.

By the following Monday, I had a game plan. I requested a meeting with her by Zoom, and we agreed to meet the next day. I was incredibly nervous. I wanted the money back I had paid for that next round of consultations because no work had been delivered. But I had been roped into the situation so deeply that I'd made a huge mistake; there was no contract in place. The chances of getting any money back were slim, and I knew it.

She also had my work, which made me nervous. I felt exposed and vulnerable. I wanted to tell her I was concerned for her mental health and encourage her to seek help. But I was afraid of the consequences that might have for me.

I tried to strike a balance and go with a portion of the truth. I began by telling her I had decided to go in a different direction with the book and that I wanted to work with an editor with more experience in my field. She was clearly caught completely off guard.

After some unproductive back-and-forth, she lashed out, going for the jugular. She said I wasn't really a very good writer after all. She used my request for a partial refund to say that I had no understanding of how anything in the industry worked. She played on my emotions, using very personal information she had about me from reading my story to try to manipulate me into feeling obligated to work with her. It was a very unpleasant conversation.

The more I listened to her, the angrier I felt. I was sad for her, as she clearly wasn't well. And I was furious because I felt deeply hurt by some of the things she said. But I was also angry with myself because I'd played a role in allowing the situation to get to this point.

After the call ended, she bombarded me with text messages throughout the rest of the day, reiterating the hurtful and manipulative things she'd said during the call. She quoted parts of my book back to me, calling me a hypocrite.

At the end of the day, I wrote an email to end contact with her. I summarized my position, trying to maintain professionalism while being compassionate. I reiterated my request for at least a partial refund, since no work had been done, and I asked that she not contact me again.

This is still a recent and painful experience for me to dissect. However, it's such a good example of what can happen when we don't have clear expectations and make assumptions in our public relationships that I decided to include it.

Without a contract in place, there were no defined expectations of what would happen in the case of separation or dispute. There was no defined recourse I could follow to get any money returned. There was nothing in place to protect my writing.

When the editor first began using terms of endearment with me, I should've drawn a boundary line. When communicating with her via text and email, I should've drawn clearer boundary lines. I shouldn't have replied during hours when I wasn't willing to be in contact. There are plenty of ways in which she also blurred and crossed lines between what was appropriate in public life and what needed to remain private.

The thing that made this difficult to see coming was the slow creeping nature of those blurring lines. That's pretty common. It's fine until it's not, as my wife is fond of saying. The frog doesn't try to hop out of the pot if the water is just gradually getting hotter. And, eventually, it's too late.

"But I want them to like me"

One of the most common reasons for blurring the lines between our public and private lives is the need to be liked. It's a human need. Even the prickliest of people I've met over the years care at some level about being liked. The trouble comes from not maintaining the right balance between being liked and being respected.

I've worked with a client for a while now who has struggled to find this optimal balance. She took on a management role with a technical team during the early months of the COVID-19 pandemic shutdown. While her background isn't technical, she was well-qualified for her position. However, self-doubt plagued her from the beginning. She felt, as many new managers I've worked with do, that her role was to always know more than her team about what they were supposed to do. That wasn't possible in her situation, and it unnerved her.

Her team was all male, which further intimidated her. I encouraged her to get to know them as people in order to build trust. At first she resisted talking to them about anything not specifically related to the tasks they were working on. She wouldn't turn her camera on for online meetings when they were all working remotely. She was perceived as distant and disconnected, which distressed her. I encouraged her again to try a few simple things to build trust and rapport with them. One of her team members was struggling with remote working more than the others and needed more contact, so she decided to start there.

Once she began reaching out more, things shifted in those relationships. The team members' perceptions of her changed, and she found she liked being liked. However, her confidence was still low because of not having technical expertise herself.

When problems inevitably surfaced in various projects the team was developing, she was hesitant to hold "the guys" accountable. The gains she'd made in building better relationships with them made her feel like they'd go back to not liking her if she called them out whenever something wasn't working. Her lack of technical expertise only added to her hesitation. She suffered from feeling like she didn't have what it took to be able to effectively lead her team—a classic example of what it means to feel like "not enough."

Things came to a head when one member of her team was clearly not performing. It got so bad that she realized she was going to have to fire him. Feeling responsible for his lack of success, she dragged her feet on taking action—until another team member started making comments about it, having noticed her hesitation to hold anyone accountable. The realization that her inaction was threatening her credibility helped her follow through on firing the nonperformer.

For several weeks afterward, she worried about the whole situation. She wanted to understand exactly where things had gone wrong to avoid repeating the same mistakes. Looking back, she realized one thing she hadn't done with anyone on her team was lay out clear expectations. Assuming her team would know what to do and would ask if they didn't, she thought they would perform their jobs without any real oversight from her. She had believed her lack of technical expertise meant she didn't have anything to contribute to their success. Coupled with enjoying being liked by them, these factors led her to avoid uncomfortable conversations with them. The man she had to fire had taken her laid-back approach to mean he didn't really have to work any harder than he wanted to.

Once she was able to see how these factors had created the perfect storm that led to her having to fire someone, she was determined not to let the situation repeat. Since then she's been working on setting clearer expectations and making no assumptions with her team members. She has realized that once they agree to expectations, it gets a lot easier to hold them accountable. This has allowed her to strike a better balance between being liked and being respected.

We're quick to blur the lines between our public and private lives. Often we don't even recognize the distinction, which can lead to inappropriate expectations of the relationships we're in.

The symptoms are everywhere: politicians kissing babies, Facebook making sure you know when it's everyone's birthday (even those of people we don't know in real life or haven't seen in 30 years), and colleagues and managers who compare the office to a family.

We've developed hundreds of ways to blur the lines. It has become so ingrained in us that it can be difficult to even recognize the problem. What we do recognize is how shitty it can feel when those lines are consistently blurred.

Emotion vs. self-interest

Another client I work with has been wanting to make a move within her organization for a while now. The timing has to be right for contractual reasons, so it hasn't been a simple thing to navigate. Recently conditions became right for her to try to make her move.

She quickly recognized the benefit of getting other people to recommend her, help her, and pave the way for this move. She's in a political organization in which it's particularly critical to understand what motivates every person involved. Seeking and gaining this understanding can be viewed as self-interest,[4] which asks the question, what is at the intersection of what I care about and what you

---

[4] Self-interest has a bad rap. It's often confused with selfishness. Selfishness is the denial of others with a sole focus on oneself. The opposite is selflessness, which is the denial of self with a sole focus on everyone else. "Self-interest" was a term we used daily in the community-organizing world, but we defined it as "self among others," combining "self" with the root meaning of "inter-esse" (among others). What do you want? What do I want? Where do those things intersect so we can find common interests and goals?

care about? And if the term is understood to mean "self among others," how can we work on something that will benefit us both?

I asked my client to make a list of all the people she knows who are connected to the role she wants. She did, and quickly realized there were more than she thought. We started reviewing her list together. I asked her about each person, what their connection was to her, what their connection was to the person who would have to accept her into the new role, and what she knew about each one.

She began describing them in terms of conversations she'd had with them in which they had encouraged her to make this move. She kept saying things like, "He likes me" or "I helped him on that project, so he is indebted to me." What I wasn't hearing was much about their self-interest. In other words, how would each of them benefit from helping her get what she wanted?

When I asked her this question about her immediate boss, she was particularly perplexed. She wanted to ask for his support and said he should want to help her because she'd always taken on the work he'd asked her to, even when she hadn't wanted to or had felt someone else in the team was better suited for a particular project.

"Yes, but what would motivate him to want to help you?" I pressed.

She stared at me, surprised. "Well, he likes me," she said.

I waited.

"He should want to help me because I've been such a good worker for him."

I waited again.

She just stared at me, not seeing it.

Finally I said, "If you're such a good worker, what would possibly motivate him to want to send you to work in another department where you would no longer be working for him?"

She continued to stare. "Well, I would certainly never want to hold someone back from working elsewhere if they weren't happy on my team," she said. "Isn't that enough?"

My client was motivated by emotion. We proceeded to have a long conversation about how this plays out in her professional life, and she quickly began to see a pattern of disappointments and frustrations directly linked to operating this way.

Her boss, like many people, is motivated more by self-interest than by emotion. He wouldn't benefit in any tangible way from her move to another department. He would lose a strong member of his team who always produces high-quality work, even when she doesn't want to work on a particular project. His self-interest in this situation is squarely on keeping her.

This conversation was a huge epiphany for my client. She began listing ways that she believes her emotional perspective has hurt her professionally over the years. Her assumption and expectation had always been that her boss, and everyone else, was operating out of emotion like she was. The realization that she was wrong was eye-opening to her. It made her reevaluate every person she'd listed to help her, causing her to look at each one very differently than before. She felt empowered and clearer.

The additional benefit she's discovered by focusing on self-interest rather than emotion is the freedom she feels. She's stopped having the expectation that everyone will be offended by direct feedback or productive conflict like she'd been, which makes her much more willing to be open and direct than she was before. Subsequently, she's gotten better results for her boss and others around her.

Selfishness leads to isolation. Selflessness leads to burnout. Try operating out of self-interest. If we look closely, we may find that we already do. Embrace it. It's 100 percent appropriate in our public-life relationships.

An example of not guessing your way through it

There are many ways in which we blur the lines between our public and private lives. This results in our projecting inappropriate expectations onto people, particularly in our public lives. One of the ways these lines get blurred is with the belief that we should simply be fully ourselves with everyone at all times. While we may usually choose to show up that way for people in our private lives, the same is likely not true for most people in our public lives.

I firmly believe in being our authentic selves regardless of where we are or who we're with. However, that doesn't mean I behave the same way with my clients that I do with my friends on a weekend. We are multifaceted human beings. If we're emotionally intelligent, we're aware of how our behavior impacts those around us.

Making adjustments to help us show up the way we want to with a client doesn't make us inauthentic or fake. It makes us aware.

I first learned this important lesson in my community-organizing days when I was working in metropolitan Cleveland as the executive director of a community organization. When I recruited a Baptist church in East Cleveland to join the organization, their pastor, Rev. Dr. Hunter, quickly became involved in the organization with other clergy members. He was a rising star.

Pastor Hunter is a quiet man. He is much older than I am, and he's a Black man who hails from the Deep South. He and his family have experienced plenty of racism. Whenever I talked with him, I was conscious of how I chose my words and how I interacted with him. I deeply respected Pastor Hunter and never wanted to do or say anything to offend him. When I visited him, I slowed down to match his pace. I never interrupted or cut him off, and I did not swear.

One day when we were still getting to know each other, we rode together to an event in Youngstown, about an hour and a half away from Cleveland. We talked about many things, including our back stories on how we were each raised. I loved listening to his stories. He was a great storyteller, taking the listener right into the moment. At one point we got onto the subject of women in the pulpit. Pastor Hunter didn't approve of women in the pulpit. He had very clear views about what he understood to be God's intentions when it came to the roles women should play in the church. This extended to the role he felt women should play in the home. He didn't believe women should speak out if they disagreed with their husbands. He also didn't believe they should hold leadership positions.

As I listened, I started to worry. I had begun to relax around him with our growing interactions. He had recently agreed to cochair the organization's Clergy Caucus with a very liberal, white Presbyterian pastor from neighboring Cleveland Heights, and he knew I was the executive director of the organization. I wasn't sure how to react to what he was saying about women. So I said nothing.

I called a trusted fellow organizer named Evans Moore (you'll hear more about him in the next chapter), whose insight I valued. I knew he'd be totally honest with me and that I could ask him anything. Telling him about my conversation with Pastor Hunter, I expressed my concern about how to continue working with him, given his views. I told him I thought that in telling me his views, Pastor Hunter must be passing me a subtle message about my leadership.

Evans listened, and then laughed at my assumption. He told me I was acting like Pastor Hunter was the first Black man I'd met and that I needed to pull my head out of my ass. While I willingly listened and didn't discount what he was saying, I admitted I wasn't sure what his point was.

Evans asked me to think about what I wanted from Pastor Hunter. What was my self-interest in working with him? What was his self-interest in working with me and with the organization? Once he refocused me on those two questions, it became clearer to me. The fact that Pastor Hunter had even shared his perspective with me at all wasn't a warning; it was a sign and message that he trusted me.

When Evans asked me how I'd reacted in the moment, I told him I'd held very still, probably holding my breath, and nodded noncommittally. He affirmed that it was a good choice.

Experiencing this exchange with Pastor Hunter was the first time I became truly conscious of how I shifted between different parts of my authentic self depending on whom I was with. I wasn't lying about who I was or falsely pretending to agree with Pastor Hunter's views, but I also wasn't picking a fight with him about his views or trying to convince him they were wrong. That wasn't in my self-interest. It only would've caused him to rethink his membership in an organization that apparently didn't have room for more than one view.

Pastor Hunter wasn't criticizing my role, my leadership, or anything aimed at me. He wasn't trying to change me or challenge me in any way. He was sharing his perspective and trusting me to hear him. Once I was able to see that, thanks to Evans, I interacted with Pastor Hunter with more confidence. I maintained my respectful demeanor as I continued to meet him where he was. He eventually became the president of my board. We worked successfully and closely together until I retired from organizing and moved back home to Michigan. I'm honored to say I went with his blessing.

The number one distinguishing feature between public and private relationships is what you're seeking. In private relationships, you seek to be loved, want to be your whole self without wearing any masks, and operate more on emotion. In your public relationships, you'll do well by seeking to be respected, appropriately filtering your authenticity based on your audience, and operating out of self-interest. When you keep those lines clear, public life gets a lot easier.

Chapter 8

ASSUMPTIONS CAUSE PROJECTIONS

To "project" is defined by Lexico as "to transfer or attribute one's own emotion or desire to another person, especially unconsciously."[5] Projections are caused by assumptions. Once they're out there, they can take on a life of their own and not even be recognizable as assumptions. They simply become accepted as "true."

Projections show up in several ways. In the more harmless examples, projected expectations can cause us to live vicariously through someone else's experience. In the more damaging examples, we project our assumptions about what motivates another person to behave a certain way.

---

[5] Lexico, s.v. "project (trans. v. 4.3)," accessed June 6, 2022, https://www.lexico.com/en/definition/project.

That projection leads to labeling, and labels can lead to being marginalized. That's as true at work as it was on the playground.

Projections can have long-lasting effects. A child who behaves in inappropriate ways can get labeled as "difficult" or "bad." Other family members may pick up on that label and use it with that child as well. The child's label can follow them to school and create an expectation with teachers of further "bad" behavior. The label can even follow the child into adulthood.

Projected fear and bias have led to entire groups in our society being marginalized and abused. People within a group become aware of those projections in various ways. The projections can lead to members of the group experiencing self-doubt and create harmful cultural narratives, promulgated primarily by people outside of the group and doing untold damage to those within it.

But that doesn't have to be the end of the story, even when it starts that way. We can recognize projections as assumptions, ask more questions, look more closely, and test the merits of those assumptions. When we find out we're wrong, we can choose to change the next part of the story.

Is that damned glass half-full or half-empty?

My mother was a product of her upbringing, as all of us are. Unfortunately, her upbringing was undertaken by a man she didn't recognize when he came back into her life. Her father had gone to fight in World War II when she was a baby. He was a German native who had fled from the threat of a concentration camp to the safety of the US. Shortly after marrying an American citizen a few years later and receiving his US citizenship, he was drafted. He went back to the continent he'd only recently fled to fight against his own countrymen.

He came back with injuries and severe PTSD, which, because this was back in 1947, went undiagnosed. To my then five-year-old mother, he was terrifying. He made it clear she wasn't up to his impossible standards from the moment he returned. Though some of his hostility turned toward his son, born after his return, my mother remained his favorite mark because she spoke up more, making herself an easier target.

The consequence relevant here was that she lived in fear of never measuring up. She held herself and those around her to very high standards and seemed to live her life with her father sitting on her shoulder, whispering in her ear that she was doing everything all wrong. She lived with an enormous fear of failure that immobilized her at times. There were clear gender disparities in her own past, so while my brother sometimes received her wrath, I was far more often her target:

"You can't play soccer! You will get hurt! You are a musician, and you will break your fingers and not be able to play."

"Why would you choose Alma College? It's nearly three hours from home! How will you know what to do out on your own? You need to go to Wayne State so you can live at home."

"You're going where?! To Central America? I think not! That's far too dangerous a place. You'll get a disease!"

Thankfully, these "warnings" about all the dangers I faced by living life were interspersed with acknowledgments of my successes. My mother loved me fiercely, a fact I recognized in full only after her death in 2020. Although I felt anger, resentment, and the tiniest bit of relief that my own fears must be warranted when my mother fought my choices, I pushed back hard against her and ended up winning most of those battles.

My mom began projecting her fears and desires for how I should live my life onto me from the moment I was born. Many parents do, but she gave voice to hers on a daily basis. She was most afraid of not being in control, so that came out most often and had a huge impact on me. I still struggle with the fear of not being in control, but it's a lot better than it was in the first half of my adulthood.

As I mentioned in the intro to this chapter, projection involves transferring our own thoughts or feelings to someone else, usually unknowingly. My mother admitted in later years that she was living vicariously through my experiences. She said I was braver than she'd ever been, and she was constantly in awe of my willingness to do new things. She projected her fears of my failure or pain onto me because living vicariously also meant she was taking on the pain of any setbacks I experienced. Conversely, she was the first to crow to her friends in celebration of my successes. She would get very angry with me if I posted any sort of announcement of success on social media without first telling her. My victory was her victory.

Once I had kids, I projected my own desires onto them to be nice to each other and have the kind of relationship I'd never had with my brother. I'd say things like, "You took Joe's toy right out of his hand. Look at him crying. How would you feel if he had done that to you?"

This kind of projection happens in relationships of all kinds, including relationships in the workplace. It shows up in statements we make to others when we've already decided how the other person should feel or behave because we've projected our own emotions or desires onto them:

"I can't tell Susan how I really feel about what she said. It will hurt her feelings and lead to a conversation I'm not ready to have."

"I can't ask Robert to take on one more thing. His plate is already so full. I'll just do it myself."

Yet another version of projection occurs when we see a place or person through someone else's eyes. For example, just as my wife and I had decided to sell our farm and move, a colleague visited. "This is such a beautiful place! So peaceful, so quiet. So much space. How could you ever want to leave it?"

But what happens when we get it wrong? We might think we're looking at things from another perspective, but we're still not seeing the full picture. We become "projectors," putting our own fears and assumptions onto someone else. As the saying goes, there are three sides to every story: our version, the other person's version, and the truth.

Going back to my previous examples, Joe, the crying child, had snatched the very same toy from his brother, Sam, just a few moments before. The one who provoked tears from the other was simply the one who got caught. The crying is what brought adult attention to the matter. Did I miss the mark in trying to get Sam to see Joe's perspective without encouraging Joe to do the same for Sam?

The woman who doesn't want to hurt Susan's feelings has suffered significant hurt feelings herself from Susan's previous outbursts. Her assumption that Susan will respond badly to her feedback is based on her own perspective and fears about the encounter. Would Susan see it differently?

The assumptions about Robert's workload may be denying Robert a chance to learn something new and grow. He might be hoping for an opportunity to work on something else. We don't know because we didn't ask.

As for the colleague who visited my farm and appreciated all its charm and beauty, she had never cared for a sick animal while also caring for a sick child. She hadn't had to go out into every kind of weather to feed and water all the animals, regardless of being sick herself or just bone-tired. She hadn't asked what was causing us to sell the farm. She was simply struck by the beauty of it and assumed that was enough.

In all scenarios, there's a missing perspective that could bring a more balanced view. Are we willing to try to see it? Are we willing to make sure that it's heard? Or are we simply more comfortable projecting our own assumptions and fears onto the situation?

This is the stuff that communication mishaps are made of. I have my take on what happened, and you have your take on what happened. We both make assumptions about the other's position and feelings. We project those fears and assumptions onto the other person and then, based on those assumptions, make decisions about what we think the other person can handle hearing. We choose not to share something that could potentially hurt, offend, or upset the other person, even though it would give greater understanding.

We need to be more worried about helping each other see the other's perspective and less worried about the potential for conflict. If we're willing to stick with the conversation, we can usually find a way to get through it. Those hard conversations often lead to an even stronger relationship and clearer path forward together.

We must also be willing to engage. Sometimes it's hard. Sometimes it's uncomfortable. It won't always go smoothly. It might not end well, at least temporarily. But if we aren't willing to genuinely seek to understand one another's perspectives, how can we hope to find common ground and find solutions?

What does she really want?

As I mentioned earlier, one way we project our fears and assumptions onto other people comes in the form of labeling. We've all met people in our workplaces who get labeled "difficult" or "hard to work with." Maybe even "gatekeeper."

We are judgmental, we humans. We're quick to take someone at face value and slap a label on them. Women get labeled the fastest. This has been both my personal experience and what I've directly observed. But no one is immune from being unjustly or inaccurately labeled.

If someone is hesitant to share information quickly, they are labeled a gatekeeper and not a team player. If someone seems to be guarding certain materials, they are labeled a control freak and not a team player. If they don't say anything in meetings, they are assumed to be in agreement. If they raise concerns later, they are judged for not having spoken up sooner.

And the list goes on.

We don't bother to stop and figure it out. We don't ask enough questions. We don't slow down long enough to reflect on the situation. And we don't look beyond the symptoms to understand the root cause of the challenging behavior. Instead, we project our assumptions based on our judgments right onto the other person.

A coaching client of mine (let's call her Marge) put this to the test with a woman who works in her plant (we'll call her Jane) and guards a specific piece of equipment as though it's her personal property. Jane routinely refuses to allow other people to use the equipment or even touch it. She causes most people to go to great lengths to bypass her because she's so unpleasant to talk to about this equipment.

Marge initially fell into the same pattern as everyone else at the plant. She labeled Jane as difficult, not a team player, entitled, and a gatekeeper. Every time she knew she was going to have to interact with Jane, Marge braced herself, expecting a negative outcome. This expectation most certainly affected her attitude and approach, which generated a negative result with Jane.

This was a situation that bothered Marge, and we discussed it in our coaching sessions. Marge began to recognize the cycle they were trapped in and decided to try to figure out what was causing Jane to act this way. What was at the root of it? What did Jane really want?

After reflection, Marge hypothesized that all Jane wanted was to be valued and respected. She wanted to feel like she was important. She wanted to be seen. Marge chose her approach accordingly, and Jane responded beautifully. She not only insisted that Marge use the equipment, but also offered to order another piece of it to keep in the other location where Marge works more often. The experience Marge gave Jane of feeling seen, heard, and valued has had lasting effects. Jane continues to communicate with Marge in a very different way than she does with other people.

Win-win.

When we project our fears and assumptions onto one another, it rarely leads to productive interactions. The collective effect of everyone in a workplace projecting similar negative assumptions onto one person can lead to that person becoming marginalized. Depending on that person's hardwired nature and personality, such assumptions may subdue them to silence, cause them to pull back from healthy interactions with others, decrease their productivity, and eventually leave the company. Projection can also go in the other direction, as it had with Jane, so that the person becomes aggressive, defensive, angry, and frustrated to the point of engaging in behavior that potentially sabotages the success of others.

Taking time to reflect on what assumptions we're making about a person we're struggling to work productively with can give us insights about what's really going on. And if we don't know, we can always try asking them some questions.

Cultural backlash

One of the most effective group projections of all time has been through our education system and the cultural narrative it spreads. For decades, the projections of white cisgendered heterosexual men have prevailed. The celebrations of "triumphs" over non-white, non-heterosexual, non-cisgendered male groups (a.k.a. everyone else) is written clearly in the history books used to teach most school-aged kids.

This narrative has pervaded the center of mainstream culture and shows up in a broad variety of ways. On the mostly harmless side, the men I encounter out in the world who don't know me project their assumption that I'm physically weak. They offer to (and sometimes insist on) carrying things for me or moving "heavy" chairs for me.

On the very harmful end of the spectrum, men exert control over women, people of color, and the LGBTQ+ community in far more serious, alarming, and sometimes deadly ways.

The projection of fear of losing control is clearly at the center of this narrative. Power historically comes from control. Losing control is terrifying. The public discourse reflecting the growing widespread awareness of these disparities is increasingly robust. That gives me hope. The more people talk about these issues and the myriad examples of how they show up, the harder it will become for the broader population to ignore.

In following and reading more people who aren't like me, I continue to be alarmed and embarrassed by the ways in which these projections are deeply ingrained in everyday life. This speaks to the second part of that definition of projecting: "to transfer or attribute one's own emotion or desire to another person, *especially unconsciously.*" I won't speak for anyone else, but I know my own intentions are never nefarious toward, for example, other races. But I've become aware of ways in which I've been guilty of unconsciously projecting my fear. Let me properly introduce you to Evans Moore.

An example of not guessing your way through it … in the end, anyway

By the end of 1999, I'd been in community organizing for two years. I was getting better at meeting people where they were and remembering that I wasn't there to save anyone. I was there to challenge them to save themselves. But I wasn't immune to fear and bias.

I met Evans when I went to Erie, Pennsylvania, to facilitate some training with the leaders of their community-organizing group. At 26, I was one of the youngest organizers, and he was about the same age. He was loud, more than a little arrogant, and appeared unafraid to take up space in whatever room he entered. I was immediately both drawn to and afraid of him. I was drawn to his charisma and the way he easily interacted with people in the room and was afraid of his arrogance and apparent confidence. I was the young star in the organizing network and wasn't ready to be replaced by someone new. I was sure there was room for only one of us.

Pete, the executive director in Erie, was an older, seasoned organizer whom I knew well. He had recruited Evans and wanted my assessment of him. We all went back to Pete's house to talk after the training. I'd been an organizer long enough to know I couldn't admit my fear of this young man, so I covered it with bluster and projection.

"He's a loudmouth," I told Pete in the car on the way back to his house. "He seems like he likes clowning around more than anything else."

Pete stared at me for a second and then burst out laughing. "Who are *you* calling a loudmouth?" he sputtered. "That's rich!" He continued to laugh as my face burned. Then he stopped laughing and gave me a hard look.

"Maybe you should try having a conversation with him before you gauge his commitment to social justice," he nearly growled, catching me by surprise with the sudden change. I immediately felt even more embarrassed. "He's walked a longer road than you ever will."

Now I felt not only embarrassed but angry. And indignant. I felt self-righteous about the difficulties of my own path. The language of bias and privilege we have now wasn't common back then, but that was exactly what I was experiencing.

Evans is a Black man. I am a white woman. It doesn't matter how many difficulties either of us faces in our path. His road will always be more difficult simply because he's Black. I knew that, but I didn't want it to be true, so I pretended it wasn't.

I decided to go on the offensive. When we had settled into Pete's living room, I glared at Evans and caught him off guard. "Why do you think you deserve to be an organizer?" I asked him bluntly.

He looked at me, surprised but not really, and I saw wisdom and weariness in his young face. My face immediately flushed as I realized how rudely I came across. He smiled at me slowly. "Nice to meet you, too," he said.

Thanks to his maturity and easygoing nature, we were able to overcome that rocky start with a longer, more productive conversation. I challenged him about his path, his struggles, and his willingness to embrace all of that to make him a great organizer. Evans is very smart and very confident. As we talked, I began seeing how we could help each other be more successful, rather than seeing him as competing with me.

I'm clear that it was only because of Evans's nature and style that we were able to move past that uncomfortable beginning. He's made jokes about my blunt style in the years since. When I went through a particularly tough time in the organization, Evans was my fiercest defender and very protective of me. He became like an older and wiser big brother, even though we were about the same age. His path has never been easy, but he has achieved great things in every role he's taken on. He's not done yet, not by a long shot. As I write this book, Evans is a trainer and national field coordinator for the Legal Defense Fund's Thurgood Marshall Institute. I'm grateful to still call him a brother and trusted colleague to this day.

We always have an opportunity to do better. Recognizing when we've assumed or projected our own shit onto someone else creates an opportunity. Evans didn't call me out directly that day, but he sure has over the years. I've called him out, too. Rather than seeing that behavior as confrontational, we both see it as a sign of investment. Care enough about those around you to invest in helping them get better. Allow them to do the same for you. We all grow together.

Chapter 9

ASSUMPTIONS AFFECT OUR ABILITY (AND WILLINGNESS) TO PUSH BACK

When my kids were little, my older son fell into the trap many young kids do of wanting to control what his little brother was doing. I found a simple graphic on the internet at the time and hung it on our refrigerator to help us all. It showed an inner circle listing ways a person can exercise control. It included "my attitude, my effort, my behavior, my thoughts, my actions." A second outer circle showed things outside of a person's control. It included "other people's attitudes, other people's efforts, other people's behavior, other people's thoughts, other people's actions."

My son struggled against an assumption that because he was older than his little brother, he should be able to control the younger one's actions. I'm not sure if that's an oldest child syndrome (I'm a youngest), but I've met many people in my own life who have tried to control what I say, do, think, and feel. When they do, my own set of assumptions creeps in: I'm not allowed to push back; I'll be called a bitch if I speak out; I'll be in danger if I speak freely.

Accurately discerning the difference between avoiding real danger and holding back only because of my own head trash is hard sometimes. "I don't want to be judged or too uncomfortable. I don't want to make anyone else feel too uncomfortable. Am I really qualified to speak up? Am I worthy? Maybe I don't have anything of value to offer. I should stay quiet and small. That's what people prefer."

Yuck.

This remains a challenge I struggle with regularly, sometimes daily: learning to find the balance of when it's important and safe to speak up and push back and when it's not.

Take no for my answer. Please.

In 2016, my wife and I bought a farm in the rural town where her siblings and parents all lived. We had 22 acres, a beautiful old barn, a carriage house, pastures, and a sprawling old farmhouse that was originally built in 1862. We were located on a dead-end road, the last farm before a final mile of fields and forests ended at a river. It was peaceful and quiet with beautiful views. We thought it might be our forever home.

In addition to being our home, the farm was part of our business. We'd created a line of workshops in which clients partnered with horses for an unforgettable and unconventional day of experiential learning. We owned a small herd of horses and had the space to hold small workshops. The downside was our location, an hour from a couple medium-sized cities and 90 minutes from both the Detroit metro area and Ann Arbor.

Prior to buying the farm, we'd spent three years living in Ann Arbor. I'd built some great professional relationships and partnerships there during that time, and when we moved, I kept in touch with many of these acquaintances. One of them was a man we'll call Fritz. A financial adviser and investor, Fritz owned his own firm that was unconnected to any of the traditional agencies. I'd gotten to know him and admired his outspoken style. He dreamed very big and had invited me to participate in a couple of projects, but they had fizzled out after a short run.

When he came with his wife to visit the farm, we got to talking about possibilities. I've always had a secret (not anymore) desire to own a bed and breakfast. We toyed with the idea of somehow converting our farmhouse into one, but with middle school-aged kids, we weren't sure that would work for several years to come while they were at home.

Fritz jumped on this idea during our dinner and thought we should build a separate retreat center. We enjoyed brainstorming possibilities over a couple bottles of wine. It was exciting to talk about, but after Fritz and his wife left, Dani and I agreed that the expense would never be recouped from such an investment. The area we were in just wasn't a destination, nor were there enough businesses nearby to support a retreat center. It felt like a huge gamble.

About a week later, Fritz called and wanted to talk more about the idea. He was convinced it was brilliant and that he could make our business "next level." I shared my wistful wish that it could be possible and our reservations about the significant risk associated with it. We ended the call with Fritz encouraging me to keep thinking about it.

Fritz called again several times in the weeks after that. I was often in the middle of something else when he called, so I didn't answer. We played some phone tag and then finally spoke a few weeks later. He reiterated his conviction that the retreat center was viable. He even went so far as to say he had some possible leads on financing. He encouraged me to call an institution to get pre-approved. His enthusiasm was infectious. I didn't come right out and squash the idea, but I also didn't agree to move forward. I reiterated our doubts, and he reiterated his encouragement to keep thinking about it and looking into possibilities.

It felt like a lot of pressure. Dani and I continued talking about the idea but became even more convinced that the risk substantially outweighed the possible reward. I finally told Fritz more firmly that we weren't interested in pursuing it. I thanked him for his belief in us and his support and told him the timing just wasn't right.

In the coming weeks, Fritz called several times. I ignored his calls, feeling badgered. I wasn't sure why he was pushing this so hard. I was busy trying to build a network in our new local area along with maintaining relationships in Ann Arbor. I didn't want to spend any more energy on Fritz's idea.

A couple of months after our last conversation, I received a nasty voice mail from Fritz. He accused me of being ungrateful and unprofessional and said that although I claimed to be a professional in human communication, here I was ignoring him and being closed off to ideas. He called my coaching skills into question in a way that hit my vulnerabilities.

I tried to ignore Fritz and what he had said, but the voice mail apparently wasn't enough for him. He took to social media and assaulted me there. He stopped short of naming me, but his posts were clearly about me. Anyone who knew me would know they were about me. I got calls from mutual professional friends asking what was going on. Fritz even had his wife post the same attacks. It infuriated me, but I held back on engaging.

At the same time, I was going through some very difficult issues on the home front. My mother had been diagnosed with early signs of dementia. My father wanted to move with her from their home of 42 years in Detroit to our carriage house. Dani and I were in agreement that it needed to happen, but we were all fighting with my mom the whole way. No one could cut me to my core like my mom could, may she rest in peace, and I felt like I was generally in a bit of a vulnerable state. Fritz's attack sent me straight into impostor syndrome territory.

Fortunately I had a great community around me. Some of my Ann Arbor contacts remained in touch, so I asked them if they'd noticed any changes in Fritz's behavior. They said they had. He was quite a character and was well known around the area. They said he seemed louder and angrier than normal and that he had stopped attending some of his regular events. I didn't tell them anything specific about my own experience, just that I'd had a disturbing conversation with him and wondered if he was doing okay.

At this time, I was also meeting new people in the area near where we'd settled. Engaging with them snapped me out of my impostor syndrome thinking. The more distance and time I put between Fritz and me, the better I felt. I haven't interacted with him in over five years now.

I've been told throughout my life that I'm too much. I'm opinionated and don't often hold back from sharing what I'm thinking, as you've read throughout this book. I spent a lot of years feeling bad about my nature, and I still struggle with it occasionally. But I've also learned to see the assets of it.

Because he knew me well enough, Fritz probably never assumed I could be bullied into taking this risk. However, he didn't take my attempts to politely say no and move on seriously. He assumed that if I wasn't coming out strongly against it, there must still be room for changing my mind.

My head trash gets in my way sometimes. It makes me think that other people who are talking are more qualified to speak up than I am. It undermines my confidence and makes me want to be liked rather than respected. And that means I avoid saying things that might make others feel uncomfortable or disappointed.

Speaking up for myself (finally) in a stronger way didn't result in a happy outcome in terms of my relationship with Fritz. But it resulted in a much more important outcome in terms of my relationship with myself. I made my voice heard, even when it wasn't what he wanted to hear. I was true to myself. And that's more important than responding the way someone else wants me to.

"I literally just said that"

Plenty of people travel the road of life differently than I do. I don't pretend to have all the answers, but I always engage and try to meet the other person where they are. Another coaching client of mine sees it very differently.

My client is a director and in one of the top three positions in her company. Let's call her Vanessa. She has a master's degree in her field and 20 years of experience. Most of the top director and VP positions are held by men in her organization, including her counterpart in the same position.

The president of the company knows her value. He seeks her input on a one-on-one basis regularly and seems to respect her opinion. But that doesn't often carry over into meetings involving more than the two of them. When Vanessa meets with her male counterpart and the president together, she notices significant differences in how the president chooses his tone and words depending on whether he's addressing her or her counterpart. Her ideas are often dismissed, sometimes literally waved away with a hand gesture, while the president seems to hang on every idea coming from her male counterpart.

Vanessa experiences this level of disregard and disrespect from some others on the leadership team as well. She's clearly the reigning expert on matters related to her area, but her suggestions are routinely dismissed without discussion or consideration, and people often speak over her in meetings.

She had a strong relationship of trust with another director (a man) who also noticed how she was being treated, and they decided to do a little test. Vanessa put forward a suggestion addressing a problem happening in her area of responsibility and expertise. It was dismissed. Five minutes later, her fellow director, who oversees a different stage of the process, put forward the exact same suggestion. The suggestion, coming from him, was embraced, discussed, and adopted. He was credited with the idea.

There are many more examples Vanessa has shared with me over time. When I ask her why she doesn't push back more, she laughs uncomfortably because that would be so counterintuitive to her nature. She values peace and harmony more than making sure her voice is heard. Knowing that that's the kind of working environment she values but clearly isn't in right now, I've asked her why she stays. She shrugs it off, saying it wouldn't be any better anywhere else, it's the nature of being one of the few females in leadership in a male-dominated company, she couldn't make the same amount of money somewhere else, and she doesn't care. She has every excuse in the book for not making a move, and she seems to fully believe every one of them. I don't buy it.

The head trash Vanessa lives with comes from a lifetime of survival. She's been through some life-altering experiences, and I think they've caused her to believe she doesn't deserve better. She doesn't see her own value. She doesn't realize how much she has to offer and what an asset she'd be to a company that would appreciate her.

Assumptions plague us internally at least as much as they wreak havoc externally—assumptions about our own worth and value, about our "right" to speak up for ourselves, about what we "deserve." Some people go in the opposite direction, assuming they deserve more than what they've got, even at the expense of others. They often do harm to others, especially historically marginalized groups.

Vanessa is an example of the former group, assuming she's not good enough, smart enough, or worthy of better treatment. These assumptions keep her immobilized, afraid to step out and take a risk, unwilling to try anything new.

I know there are lots of people out there who operate this way. But I have to be honest, it baffles, perplexes, and upsets me. What emboldens bullies more than anything else? Getting away with bullying someone. What makes it easier to keep overlooking the quieter ones? When they don't speak up. What allows assumptions to persist that misogyny, racism, and other forms of discrimination are acceptable? A lack of pushback.

Fuck that.

We need to support each other to keep pushing back. We have to keep encouraging each other to reject poor treatment as "fine." We must take a more proactive role in standing together in public places and not just in the quiet places where our friendships and allyships reside. When we don't push back against assumptions about our own worth, we lose. Every. Time.

Stumbling on pronouns

In 2012, I was leading many in-person team work-shops. About half of them consisted of fun, high-energy team-building exercises, and the other half focused more on skill development in a boardroom setting. The team-building workshops never went more than two to three hours, but the skill-building ones usually lasted a day or two. I did a lot of my work at that time as a third-party contractor, with contracts that were "one and done." I didn't have much of a relationship with a point of contact beyond clarifying logistics and outcomes for the session, and I had no contact with the members of the team I'd be working with prior to walking into the workshop that first day.

I enjoy working with teams very much. What was chal-lenging about working in that way was the lack of any initial connection or trust with the group. I had to work at quickly establishing those things from the beginning. I chose to do this by sharing things about myself. Telling stories is a great way to make a point while also building rapport.

I had settled into my life with my wife at that point. We'd been together for four years, and we'd gotten married in 2011. We live in Michigan where same-sex marriage was still illegal at that time, so we took our kids with us to Iowa and eloped. Attitudes about same-sex marriage were still dicey at that point, so I was careful what I shared in my public life about my personal relationship.

During one of the workshops, I started telling a story about one of my kids. It was a great illustration of the point I was making about how we learn. Being a comfortable speaker and having conducted that workshop many times, I didn't think too much in advance about which stories I would use. I had a few in my arsenal, and this one about my kid was one I'd told before. As I got into telling it, the group engaged. They laughed at all the right places, and I relaxed into the story. My wife was a prominent part of the real-life event I was describing, but I usually minimized her role to avoid outing myself. I assumed it might make people uncomfortable and could hurt my credibility. I assumed people would focus more on whom I loved rather than seeing me as the subject matter expert.

On this particular occasion, I wasn't paying as careful attention to how I told the story like I usually did. Before I realized it, I was talking about my "spouse" more than normal in this story and had gotten myself into a very tricky pronoun trap. It was obvious I was avoiding any pronouns that would identify her gender. I started talking faster, because that's what I do when I think things are going off the rails. It didn't help me. I looked around at the group and saw they were all watching me. I noted expressions of confusion, concern, and what I thought looked like mild amusement. I stopped, trying to figure out how to get the story back on track to the point I was trying to make.

One guy in the group said, "Do you want to just tell us the name of your husband, or is he someone famous we'll recognize?" Chuckles in the room. Some sounded uncomfortable, including mine.

"Well, the thing is, I don't have one of those," I said cautiously, feeling very nervous all of a sudden. "I have a wife."

Silence. Then the same guy said slowly, "Okay … so do you want to just tell us her name?"

"Sure," I said, laughing nervously again. "Dani. Danielle. Her name is Danielle, but we call her Dani."

Heads nodded. I took a breath and finished my story.

Why was it such a big deal to mention my wife as casually as hetero people mention their spouses? This group didn't seem to care. It didn't seem to affect my credibility the way I'd assumed it would.

My fear came from other experiences we'd had prior to that workshop. For example, we'd been asked not to hold hands or show affection in front of our nieces and nephews. The request came from other family members who told us that it created confusion for the kids and that the parents didn't want to have to explain our relationship to them. I was outraged at the time but also immediately felt shame. We hadn't displayed overt public displays of affection by any means, so this felt like a clear rejection of our relationship as normal or valid. It felt absolutely horrible to be scolded for being in love, like we were doing something wrong or immoral.

Dani and I made the decision to elope with just our kids in attendance because we wanted our wedding day to be just about us. We didn't want to ask anyone in our families to come for fear they'd take away from our focus on each other that day. When we attended a family function a week later, there wasn't a single acknowledgment of our marriage. We moved away not long after that. We felt "tolerated" but definitely not "accepted."

My assumption walking into that training room, and many others like it for a good five years after I married Dani, was that just mentioning my wife as casually as a man would mention his when telling a story would be too much of a distraction for some people in the group. I'd be accused of "flaunting" my sexuality or "promoting an agenda." Those messages were coming across loud and clear from some members of our families, the media, and many politicians. It didn't feel safe to be out publicly. To be honest, I've been asked about my marriage after a workshop, but only a few times. It's a small percentage of how often I assume it will happen.

The Supreme Court decision in 2015 making same-sex marriage legal gave me more confidence. But it also brought out the trolls and people with strong opposing opinions. Too bad. My marriage is legal. If it offends you, we shouldn't work together. When I tell stories in workshops and my coaching, I don't dwell on the fact that I have a wife instead of a husband, but I don't hide it either. I've gotten better at telling the stories that include that fact, and when it comes out, it comes out. Most people don't bat an eyelash.

An example of not guessing your way through it

As I've mentioned a few times in this book so far, I spent 1997 living in rural Nicaragua. The understanding at the beginning of my term was that I would stay for two years. I worked on a reforestation project under the guidance and umbrella of a local NGO. The director of that NGO, Arsenio, didn't care for my level of independence. He made my life more difficult than necessary, but I found ways around his roadblocks as I worked in a dozen villages with teams of "Ecological Brigades."

Several months into the first year, I did something careless and upset a powerful local business owner. When I became aware of my error, I apologized profusely, and with some time we worked it out. Life moved on. I forgot about it and focused on my work.

Several weeks later, Arsenio somehow got wind of what had happened and decided this was a great opportunity to cut my contract short. He made sure the US-based organization that had sent me heard about the incident, which was now two months past, and gave them an exaggerated version of what had really happened.

Ultimately, the home organization decided that maintaining a good relationship with Arsenio as director of this NGO was more important than me, and they pulled the plug. They made the decision to end my contract after one year instead of two. It was just a few days before Christmas, when everything in Nicaragua would be shut down for two full weeks, and I had to leave at the end of January.

The logistics of life work very differently in rural Nicaragua than they do here, especially back in 1997. There was no electricity or running water in about half of the villages where I worked. Everything had to be done by passing messages over the local radio station or sending notes on the public transport buses. Neither method was terribly reliable. I had often announced a planned visit that way, only to show up and realize no one had gotten the message.

There wasn't enough time to visit all the villages where I worked, so I decided to try to call a meeting in the central town. My hope was that the leaders I'd worked with during the year would come to town to say goodbye. We'd started doing great work together based on a two-year plan, and now it would be cut short. I was more devastated at the thought of abandoning them and that work than about anything else.

When Arsenio got wind of the meeting, he was angry. He had assumed I would hang my head in shame for being publicly called out and that I'd go quietly. He openly mocked me in front of the rest of the staff for trying to organize a meeting with the "peasant farmers," and made condescending comments about my naivete and laughed.

Village leaders didn't have a great track record for coming into town for meetings called by this NGO. He told everyone he couldn't wait to sit in my meeting and laugh when no one showed up. I was furious and embarrassed, but I was also secretly afraid he'd be right. I bit my lip and said nothing in response to his tirades.

Arsenio didn't like my independence because it meant he couldn't control me. He was nervous about who I was working with in the villages because he didn't have a great reputation with everyone. He was afraid I would build something successful without his assistance. To him, this was terrifying. Organizing people to act together meant power. The more I built, the more he perceived me as a threat.

I spread the word about my unexpected departure as best I could, by radio announcements, notes out to the villages, and word of mouth. There was no other way to get the news out. I had no way of knowing whether anyone was receiving my messages, and I received no responses. I only had time to visit a few of the closest villages. When I did, people were outraged to hear what had happened, but they were noncommittal about attending my meeting. I didn't feel confident that more than a few people would come.

When the day arrived, I took a deep breath and set out to walk the mile and a half to the outdoor covered pavilion another NGO had kindly offered to let me use. Arsenio drove past me in his truck. He didn't offer me a ride. Instead, he laughed gleefully, sure he was about to witness my humiliation, and waved to me before speeding off.

As I walked up to the pavilion, I could see there were just a few people there. They were standing around talking and greeted me warmly when they saw me. I tried to hide my disappointment and fear as I smiled at them. There was no sign of Arsenio. Soon, more people began to arrive. By the time we started the meeting, nearly 100 people were there representing all the villages where I'd worked.

To get started, I asked each village's representatives to stand and introduce themselves, as they had never all been gathered together before. As they did, they started reading letters. Some of them were illiterate, so they'd brought school-aged kids with them to read the letters they'd dictated for them to write. The letters were directed in part to me, thanking me for all the work we'd done together and for believing in them. In part, the letters were directed to Arsenio, declaring their anger that he had allowed me to be removed prematurely and hadn't stopped it from happening. I was speechless. I also couldn't stop crying.

Arsenio finally arrived about halfway through the community introductions and letters. As he came in, I saw a quick flash of disbelief on his face at the sheer number of people present. He sat down quietly to listen, and I watched his expression of disbelief turn to a combination of anger, defiance, and shame.

He had assumed I wouldn't be successful in gathering people for the meeting. He had projected his own fear of failure with the villagers onto me. Rather than helping or supporting me, a member of his team, in being successful, he had stood by ready and hoping to witness my failure.

Even though my belief in my own success hadn't been strong going into the meeting, it was important to me to nevertheless try everything I could to be successful. I was completely overwhelmed by the response. I still get emotional writing about it. I still have all the letters. It was an important moment for me, standing up for who I really was and what I'd built in those villages.

We must find the courage to speak up for ourselves. There are so many assumptions we must push back against to speak our truth:

- I'm not good enough.
- I'm not smart enough.
- Maybe they're right about me.
- I'll be judged.
- I'll make others uncomfortable.
- I'll be too uncomfortable.
- I'm not qualified.
- I'm not worthy of speaking up.
- I don't have anything to offer.
- It's safer to remain silent.

I'm calling bullshit on all of it. Even if there are elements of truth to any of those statements, who cares? That can't stop you from challenging the assumptions. Otherwise, the bullies will win.

Chapter 10

ASSUMPTIONS AFFECT OUR ABILITY TO REFLECT

As you've read the stories throughout this book, I hope you've spotted the ways in which I (often) made the mistake of getting caught up in the moment and acting on assumptions without pausing to reflect until much later. That's what we do as humans. We're in the moment and can't see the forest through the trees. Oftentimes, that means we assign blame or responsibility to the other person for a given situation going sideways.

We're too close. Assumptions make us blind to how we've messed up.

The act of stepping away and reflecting on what's happening, the direction the situation is going in, the likely outcome that will happen, and how to change course is critical. It's the only thing that allows us to question our assumptions, digest our experiences, take meaning from them, learn, and do differently next time. Reflecting allows us to dig deeper.

In this final chapter, I'm taking a slightly different approach. So far, every chapter has included mostly stories about getting things wrong with one ending story about another way to do it. Every story in this chapter starts with getting caught up in the assumption traps, stopping to reflect (sometimes by force), and then making an adjustment to course correct.

That doesn't mean the stories are any less painful and embarrassing. Please read on.

Location. location. location

In 1999, during my early organizing days in East Chicago and Hammond, Indiana, Friendship Baptist Church decided to try to reclaim the park kitty-corner to the church. Loitering and drug deals by unsavory characters had turned it into a place that local residents avoided and where neighborhood kids didn't feel safe enough to play.

We organized a community action to take place one summer evening at the park. We wanted to call attention to the problem, create a platform for church and community members to tell their stories about it, and ask the city's parks and recreation director to take action. Specifically, we had come to understand that there was money to be spent but it was going other places. We wanted a commitment from the director to invest city dollars into this park.

We'd invited the director to attend the event, along with the mayor, gathered about 50 people in the park, and began our community action. None of the city officials we were familiar with showed up. In the crowd there was one man we didn't recognize who was mingling and looking like he was trying to blend in. We decided to carry on and give it some time.

As an organizer, I always stayed in the background. My job was to help prepare leaders to speak, organize the logistics and details of the meeting, strategize with them for the best outcomes, and do any other legwork they weren't available to do. But I never spoke in front of the group or led a public meeting. So at this particular event in the park, as per my usual habit, I wasn't at the front of the group. I was circulating around the back. Soon I noticed the man we didn't know watching me and starting to look angry. I moved closer to my leaders.

The parks and recreation director didn't show up. Neither did the mayor. The group was starting to feel unsure what to do. As I was talking quietly with the pastor and leaders off to the side, the man we didn't know approached us, looking hostile. Turning to face the man, the pastor addressed him and asked how we could help him.

The man kept staring at me and walked right up to me, getting in my face. I instinctively backed up a step, but he kept coming. I put my hands up to stop him from pushing me with his chest. We were eye to eye.

"Back off," I growled at him. "Who the hell are you, and why are you stepping up on me?"

He growled back, "Who the fuck are YOU? What's a little white girl doing out here in the 'hood? You lookin' for trouble? You tryin' to get these nice church folk in trouble?" He punctuated his words by jabbing his finger in my face.

I was scared. I had no idea who this guy was and why he seemed so angry at my presence. A couple of the leaders who were bigger than he was came closer, ready to step in if he touched me.

Several others started firing questions at him about who he was and why he was harassing us. A lot of yelling ensued. He wouldn't say where he was from or who he was representing. We suspected he might be with the city. East Chicago's mayor had been in office for many years and was rumored to be connected to the Mafia in Chicago. I felt like I was in bizarro world. *The Sopranos* was a popular television show at that time that I watched regularly, and I felt like laughing at the bravado I was witnessing right in front of me. It reminded me of Tony Soprano's exaggerated machismo. Then the man pushed me.

As soon as he shoved me, the leaders from the church stepped between us and someone put their arm around me to lead me away from him. He hadn't hurt me, but he had definitely scared me. There was more yelling and a lot of confusion.

The pastor, who was a calm and quiet man, raised his arms and spoke in a strong and powerful voice I imagined he probably used when preaching. I hadn't had the privilege of hearing it before. He called for attention and then for the church members to go back to the church. The woman who had led me away was part of the leadership, and she ushered me in that direction as well.

The silence and safety of the church was comforting. Once we were all inside, everyone began talking at once. As several women clucked over me, making sure I was alright, their motherly attention was enough to undo me, and I started to cry. That caused more clucking, hugging, and reassurance. I tried to pull myself together. I was embarrassed to be falling apart and imagined my boss, the lead organizer, scolding me for breaking down.

Everyone was trying to figure out who the man was and why he'd shown up at our event. We decided we were pretty sure he was from the city, but we couldn't figure out why he had attacked me. Someone said he'd yelled something about me, the only white person present, being at fault for no official from the city having shown up. We were all truly perplexed. Once we'd talked for a while and everyone was feeling like the excitement of the evening was over, we parted ways and went home.

The next day I went to the organizing office and talked to my fellow organizers about what had happened. The permanently angry expression on the face of my lead organizer, Paul, seemed to get even angrier as I recounted my story. Everyone except him expressed shock that I'd been shoved. He didn't say anything during the conversation, he just listened.

When I finished telling the story, I wasn't sure what to do next. I still couldn't figure out why the man's hostility had been directed at me and why he'd said it was my fault that no one from the city had shown up. That confusion bothered me more than having been pushed.

No one said anything for a minute or two. Paul still looked angry, and we could almost see the wheels in his brain turning. I asked him what he thought.

"I think that guy was right," he said.

I felt like he had just slapped me. "Are you joking?" I shot back, instantly feeling pissed off and defensive.

He barked a sharp laugh and told me to calm down and take a step back. He said I wasn't seeing the picture clearly because I was too close to it. I took a breath and tried to calm down. My mind was racing. I instantly felt sure I'd somehow messed everything up for my leaders at Friendship Baptist.

"Think about it," Paul said. "This guy didn't want to tell you who he was. You're all pretty sure he worked for the city, but he wouldn't identify himself. Your community action, by your own account, was a failure. No one was officially there from the city, you got no commitment for anything you wanted from the city, and there was no resolution to the problem, right?" His summary of the evening was painfully accurate. I nodded in defeat and said nothing.

"Why would someone who worked for the city be upset at your failure? And why would they target the one white person, who wasn't even speaking publicly, as the reason it had failed?"

I was at a loss. I didn't know. I shrugged.

"I don't think he wanted you to fail. I think he was frustrated that you failed. He assumed you were the reason for the failure because what white person would want to help a Black church in East Chicago push back against their white mayor and white parks and rec director? He assumed you had designed something to fail in order to protect the administration."

I felt slapped again. His analysis made sense. I felt nauseous. And angry.

"So what the hell are we supposed to do now?" I said, sounding desperate even to my own ears.

Paul smiled, anger glinting in his eyes. "Take the fucking fight to them." I didn't follow and frowned.

"As long as you're contained in a run-down park in East Chicago, beating your chests and yelling about inequities from there, you're not a threat," he continued. "Take the fight to them."

The director of parks and recreation didn't live in East Chicago. He lived in a wealthy, 99 percent-white suburb called Munster. We'd found that out during our discovery process while planning the event in the park. I imagined the leaders of Friendship Baptist walking through his neighborhood, speaking through a megaphone about injustices as they had in that park.

I shook my head. "No way," I said. "I'm not putting them in danger like that. Someone would call the cops on us. I'm not setting them up to be arrested."

Paul laughed, amused at my greenness. "You don't use the same tactics," he said. "Just showing up there will rattle him. Your leaders should kill them with kindness, creating no grounds on which they can get arrested."

I decided to take the idea back to the team at Friendship Baptist. When I shared Paul's analysis with them, they agreed it made sense. No one had been able to come up with any other explanation for the mystery man and his rage.

We brainstormed ideas and decided to take a drive. We piled into two vehicles and drove to Munster. Along the way we saw beautifully maintained parks with basketball courts, shiny new playground equipment, and lush grass. The leaders got inspired.

They decided to create pamphlets summarizing the facts: the rates of violence present in East Chicago parks, the nonexistent budget allotted to them, and the rundown conditions. The pamphlets included a picture of their park alongside one of a park in Munster. They also included a picture of the director of parks and recreation from the city's website and a statement that they wanted him to give the parks of East Chicago the same level of care he expected in his own children's parks. There was also a quote from the pastor about wanting the same conditions for the children of his church that were available to the children of Munster.

After printing copies of the pamphlets, we decided to go door to door in the director's neighborhood. We planned a brief speech for each doorknocker to say if they got the chance to speak to someone in person. We decided to keep our demeanor calm, polite, and respectful. Our intent was to have a conversation, increase awareness, and request that they ask their neighbor (the director) about why this was happening.

We also decided I shouldn't go with them. The leadership didn't want to give the neighbors anything to focus on other than their pamphlets and core message. They were still a little nervous about the confrontation at the park and didn't want to take any chances of a repeat. I reluctantly agreed to stay back and wait for them to return.

They came back jubilant. Everything had gone very smoothly. They'd been able to talk to a few people who'd been outside and were surprised to learn that their neighbor was the director of parks and recreation in East Chicago. Further, they were shocked to see the differences in conditions of the parks and open to hearing the stories the church leaders shared with them. Although the doorknockers had received some wary looks and skeptical responses, no one had called the police on them, and everyone from Friendship Baptist had made it back safely without incident. We considered it a success.

We could've chosen to give up after that first action in the park. We could've written off the man who showed up and got aggressive as just "crazy." We could've kept yelling through a megaphone into the wind, where no one who could make something happen would've heard us.

We also could've chosen to keep our own counsel about the incident and not asked for help in processing the experience. It was outside perspective that helped us see the situation from a totally different viewpoint. Reflecting on our experiences led to regrouping. It caused epiphanies and insights that wouldn't have happened had we not stopped to reflect.

Reflecting with my boss hadn't been pleasant. It had made me feel bad because it exposed my blind spots.

But exposing them was the only way for me to see them and decide to do something different. Being uncomfortable was a necessary part of moving beyond my assumptions about our approach and our experiences. Working through that discomfort is the only thing that allowed me to see what else might be possible.

Being willing to reflect honestly, even when it's painful, is something I've gotten more comfortable with over the years. I still make way too many assumptions in situations today, but my willingness to reflect and then course correct is the only way I know to keep moving through.

Silent fighting

I was a jerk. I had been under what some might say was a lot of stress. Nearly all of us revert to our hardwired tendencies when we're stressed out, and those default settings come screaming out in me, for sure. I like my own ideas best, so if something isn't happening the way I want it to, I can be a little tantrum-y. (It's not easy to admit this publicly, but here I am admitting it anyway.)

This behavior is hard to recognize when we're right in the middle of acting it out, but I have gotten so I can see it pretty quickly afterward. Usually. The following occasion wasn't one of those times, unfortunately.

When things didn't go well in this particular situation, I immediately started blaming the other person involved. "Why isn't she helping me? Why is she doing it like that? Why is she taking over? Doesn't she think I'm capable?"

These were all things I was screaming in my head. And yes, I'm aware of the contradictions. A few snarky comments did escape my lips, but the screaming, I'm happy to say, remained contained in my cranium.

I spent literally the rest of the day and a chunk of the next day fuming. I didn't want to talk about it. I didn't feel able to talk about it. Instead, I stomped around, avoiding eye contact, until I had cooled off. Only then was I able to have a conversation about it. Only then was I able to see what assumptions I'd made and just how wrong they were.

The other person involved in this story is as amiable as they come. She's one of those rare people (in my experience) who is quietly and supremely confident with no trace of arrogance. She simply knows what she's capable of, and she moves around in the world getting things done. She's the first to help if someone asks and the last to criticize or question (out loud) if someone does something differently than she would. If she doesn't know how to do something, she simply figures it out. She's one of the most non-offensive humans I've ever met.

And all those qualities are part of why I married her.

But sometimes, when I'm on the struggle bus, those same qualities light me the fuck on fire.

What I was unable to see when I was in the midst of this struggle was that it wasn't her fault that I was struggling. It was wholly, 100 percent mine. Once I'd calmed down and started reflecting on what had happened, I realized just how off base my assumptions had been. Then the embarrassment crept in.

I sought her out to talk about it and apologized. I asked questions to help me understand whether any of my assumptions had been even partially right. Turns out the answer was no. She also confessed to having made some incorrect assumptions. Our open dialogue cleared the air and allowed us to move forward with renewed commitment to one another to ask more questions when our tempers flared.

Why do we always need to look for someone to blame? Why don't we stop more often and look at ourselves before pointing a finger at someone else? As the old saying goes, "One finger pointing at someone else means three fingers pointing back at yourself." Why are we so quick to disregard this as truth?

My wife's confidence is amazing and beautiful. And when I have a crisis of confidence it isn't her fault, nor is it her responsibility to fix. It's mine. Period. When I metaphorically jab a finger at her, I see three other fingers coming directly back at me.

Stop for a moment and identify one thing you're blaming on someone else.

What would happen if you were to take responsibility for it?

Can you see past your feelings of hurt, sadness, anger, and so forth to understand that no one else holds the pen to your story?

If you were able to pick that pen back up and start writing again, how would you change the direction in which you're headed?

The everyday

A million things happen in everyday life that trigger our assumptions. When we let them take over and act on them, we usually experience a frustrating result. That's normal. The key is to reflect on what happened, what went wrong, and what assumption you were operating on that led you to that result.

I once got mad at my office manager because I couldn't find the draft of a critical grant proposal in the folder where I expected it to be. Tensions ran high, as did my stress level, and I yelled at her. She calmly looked at me for a moment, asked quietly if I'd like her to show me where the draft was, and then pointed me straight to it. Unable to take responsibility for my reaction in that moment due to emotion, I simply stormed out of her office.

Once I cooled off, I quickly recognized that I'd been completely at fault for how that interaction turned confrontational. I went back to her and apologized. I asked if she could organize the hard drive better than I had so that it made more sense to both of us and then give me a tour of where to find things. She immediately agreed, apologizing for having put the draft in a different folder than where I had expected it to be, and got to work.

When I came into corporate work from community organizing, I realized I was different from many other coaches and facilitators. Many people have a knack for seeing right through someone's untrue narrative. Not everyone has the courage to call it out.

I do.

This courage isn't popular all the time. I could give hundreds of examples (if not thousands) from my lifetime of hearing things like these:

"If you could just keep your mouth shut ..."

"Why do you always have to be so direct?"

"Ouch. Why you gotta call me out like that?"

After a while it wears me down. I start wondering if courage is actually more of a curse than a strength. I try to make myself less offensive. I get smaller. I try to take up less space, and I try to make less noise.

But doing those things causes a problem for me. I get frustrated. I feel like I have to try to be something I'm absolutely not. And I become resentful at feeling like I have to please others.

I was experiencing such frustration with a coaching client recently. We'd been working together for about 18 months, and I had stopped pointing out things I thought would be hard for her to hear. I was feeling beaten down from other places in my life, and this dynamic was carrying over into my work.

This client had hired me in the first place because of my courage, as do most of my clients. Now, displaying some courage of her own, she confronted me about the frustration she was sensing from me and asked me to tell her what was really going on. When I explained that I'd become frustrated from holding back so as not to offend her, she smiled at me.

"But my dear Ellen, that's exactly why I hired you."

Oh. Oh, yeah. That's right. I had brought my authentic self to our first call. And to many interactions after that. But then came that beaten-down feeling, one that periodically cycles through my life when I'm not being authentic in some part of it.

I'm getting better at recognizing when I'm changing my behavior in a way that's out of alignment with who I am. I'm remembering that I can craft a message in a way that the person receiving it can really hear me and still be true to my courage.

It really is okay to not be everyone's cup of tea. Every now and then, I forget that in the day-to-day. Something will happen, my confidence will falter, and I'll start feeling like I should try to please more people. Then something else will happen, causing me to reflect, and I'll realize what bullshit that attitude is.

In my experience, none of us take the time to do that reflecting part often enough. We're quick to write off other people as the problem. We get a little too comfortable assuming the worst—either about the other person or ourselves. We stop testing those assumptions. I wrote this book to reflect on some of the consequences these choices have had for me. The more we can build intentional reflection time into our lives, the easier it gets to avoid Assumption Land.

So now what?

When I met him in 1998, Greg was the founding director of the Gamaliel Foundation, the community-organizing network to which I later belonged. I attended "Weeklong", the leadership training I would later help facilitate. The week was used as a sort of weeklong job interview to become an organizer.

In addition to providing a venue for job interviews such as mine to take place, the goal of that week was to give leaders from communities and churches throughout the metropolitan regions where Gamaliel operated a chance to reflect—on their leadership, on their lives, and on their paths forward. On the first night of training, in the kickoff session for what promised to be a very intense week, Greg told us, "Life is a series of undigested experiences."

Reflecting on our undigested experiences was indeed intense. Rather than being a passive exercise spent in ponderous silence, it was highly interactive, with every-one actively engaging with the people around them. It was designed to make us dig deep and get in touch with our deepest self-interest (in the sense that I described in chapter 7) as well as our anger about injustice in the world. Then we were challenged about how willing we were to put that anger to use to change our communities. It wasn't for the faint of heart. I loved every minute of it.

That week was the first time I'd been challenged to reflect on my experiences, the collection of stories that make up who I am, and then put those reflections to use by taking action. Reflection was part of every step of the process.

If we want to understand our communities better, we have to talk to a lot of people to understand their perspec-tives and experiences. Then we must reflect on what we learn from them to decide what direction to propose.

I learned that if I wanted to understand a particular leader better, I had to sit down with them and get them to tell me their stories. I had to listen for their self-interest, what mattered to them, what they worried about, and what motivated them. Then I had to reflect on what I'd heard to decide how to invite them to engage.

I've also learned that if we want to understand ourselves better, we have to reflect on our own experiences. What's in the collection of stories that make up who we are? Where do we come from? What have we been through? How has it all shaped who we are and how we move through the world today? Where are we going? Why is that important to us? I learned that I had to understand my own self-interest in order to decide how to move forward.

Reflection happens all the time, on the fly and on the go. Simply processing a conversation and realizing you should've or could've said or done something differently is reflecting. But that's reflecting at a pretty superficial level. This is what I've discovered about other levels of reflection:

- *Reflecting at the end of the day is helpful.* It can be done while we're commuting home. Although now many of us work from home at least some of the time, we can still create a "commute" where we step away from work and spend a few minutes reflecting on the day before rejoining family or moving on to other things.
- *Reflecting at the end of the week is revealing.* It can help us realize any loose ends that need to be addressed the following week. We can reflect on the wins as well as the challenges of the week and what we can learn from them. It always helps me to leave my work and

enjoy the weekend more fully if I know I've evaluated where I am on things before turning out the light in my office. I almost always leave some notes on my desk at the end of the week about where I want to pick back up on Monday morning.

- *Reflecting at the end of the month is powerful.* Much like looking at the week does, reflecting for the month helps me gauge progress on my goals. It's a bigger-picture view. I can put the weeks into perspective when I reflect on the month.
- *Reflecting at the end of the quarter is eye-opening.* I need to see where I'm veering off the roadmap that I've created for myself. I need to see where I'm making progress and where I'm getting sidetracked or derailed. In this reflection, I make plans for getting back on track or adjust my goals based on information I now have that I didn't have when I last created or adjusted those goals.
- *Reflecting at the end of the year is essential.* How will we know how we've done if we don't reflect? How will we know how to adjust for the coming year?

I've created a downloadable reflection guide for you. You can find it at this link on my website: leadquine.com/reflections.

It includes questions and prompts to help you get started reflecting at whichever level feels right for you. If you feel overwhelmed by the prospect of reflecting, start small. Start by reflecting at the end of each day for a week and see what happens. Build from there.

CONCLUSION

It's worth getting confirmation on the vast majority of assumptions. The internet is full of articles and self-help resources for how to improve communication in your team, your company, or just with one problematic coworker. But reading about strategies to help you isn't enough.

Ideas are important, wonderful, and great. But they're just ideas hiding among the scribbled notes of an otherwise specific, practical blueprint for taking action.

There are probably some people out there who have an ability to hear suggestions of new behavior and simply begin implementing it. I haven't met them, but it's possible they exist. Much more common are regular folks like me who need a little (or a lot) more intentionality behind making changes.

In each chapter of this book, I've made suggestions about ways you can try this stuff out yourself. But before you take a look at your own assumptions, we need to have a heart-to-heart about how to take action. Everyone's a little different, so it's important that you be committed to trying out various strategies until you find one that works for you.

My favorite strategy involves good old-fashioned sit-down-and-think work. It could look something like this:

1. Start with one person with whom you'd like to see a change (coworker, boss, spouse, or someone else who comes to mind when you think about assumptions you've made).
2. Think about your interactions with that person and then what you don't like about those interactions. Be as specific as possible.
3. Reflect on your last difficult interaction with them and answer the following questions:
   a) What happened?
   b) How were you feeling?
   c) What did you say?
   d) What did you assume?
   e) What did they seem to assume?
   f) What did they say?
   g) How did they seem to be feeling?

There are many more questions that can develop from there, but these are a good starting point. Pay attention to which questions you can answer easily and which ones you can't without making guesses or assumptions. If you start feeling defensive as you answer the questions, pay attention to that too. Defensiveness puts us into fight/flight/freeze mode and blurs our proverbial vision. Honest reflection can't happen while we feel defensive.

Let's try another exercise. You can use the same person as you did in the first exercise, or you can pick someone new:

1. Write down (or type out) in as much detail as possible a description of the choke point with this person. (Not literally where you want to choke them, but more like the bottleneck. For the record, we do NOT want you to choke anyone.)

2. Your reflections may lead to insight about a deeper problem in the relationship. Here are a few more questions you can ask yourself to help you think about the bigger picture with this person:
   a) What level of trust do you have with this person?
   b) How are you managing conflict with them?
   c) How are assumptions affecting the relationship?
   d) What would help the relationship be more productive?

You can answer these questions on a couple of levels. Chances are, there's a gut reaction level where you want to cast all responsibility onto the other person. If you've come to a tough spot with them, you might feel too much anger or apathy to come up with a productive solution. Once you're able to move beyond that initial reaction, you have an opportunity to gain insight. Look at those detailed descriptions of the choke points you (hopefully) wrote out a few minutes ago. Think about a few concrete and specific things you could do to improve your ability to communicate with this person—small stuff; something you could say that you currently aren't saying or ask that you currently aren't asking.

Change happens in deceptively minor shifts. Big, sweeping changes rarely stick and therefore should not be the goal. Let's go one small step at a time.

What's one question you could ask next time instead of making an assumption about the answer?

What's one small thing you could do or say differently next time that might elicit a more productive reaction or result?

By always thinking about small things you can do during the next interaction, you're less likely to feel over-whelmed about being able to change the relationship and more likely to be able to do something different that will improve it.

Thank you for coming along on this ride with me. I hope my stories of how I get this stuff wrong all the time have been helpful for you. I hope you laughed and that you could see yourself in some of them. I hope you felt deep emotion, and I hope you were moved to want to do something different, even if it's something small.

I'm a real person with a real business. I'm accessible. I love to talk to people about their experiences, especially when they're looking for ways to do it better, to get it a little more "right," and are willing to just keep trying. There are lots of ways to connect with me and read content from me more regularly. I encourage you to visit my website, sign up for my monthly musings, and connect with me on social media.

Assume nothing, my friends. The saying is true. It really does make an ass out of you and me. We can do better, and we can help each other.

ACKNOWLEDGEMENTS

The journey to publishing this book was longer and stranger than I imagined it would be when I first thought I might want to write it. It never would have come into existence without a small army of talented and insightful people pushing me, cheering me on, and supporting the process, even when I ran out of steam. Here are just a few of them.

Thank you, Jared Rosen, for brainstorming with me until the idea for this collection of stories was strong enough to grow legs.

Thank you, Jenn T. Grace, for meeting me where I was—a little broken and unsure—and picking me back up to keep going. Thank you, Noël King and Nancy Graham-Tillman, for taking my raw material and making it into a much better read. Thank you, Bailly Morse and everyone in the back rooms at PYP making everything else happen. I simply would not have crossed the finish line without every single one of you.

Thank you to my early readers who were kind and generous enough to share their thoughts about this book (see them at the front of this book).

Thank you to the organizers and leaders of the various organizations within the Gamaliel Foundation network, my faith-based organizing home. You took a chance on me when I was young and unrefined. You invested in me, pushed me hard, and made me want to be the version of myself that you could see when I could not. I would not be doing this work the way that I do it if it weren't for those amazing years with you. Special thanks to those named in this book.

Thank you to my "dynamic duo" virtual administrative assistants, Karen and Beth. You keep me organized, you keep me honest, and you keep me from procrastinating beyond reason. None of this promotional stuff would have happened without you both.

Thank you to my wife and kids, who, much to my astonishment and delight, just keep on loving me through everything.

ABOUT THE AUTHOR

Ellen Patnaude

CEO & Founder, LeadQuine

Ellen Patnaude has always been fascinated by how a person's nature and nurture combined causes them to interact with the people around them. She is a Detroit native and graduated from Alma College with a

BA in Biology & French. She thought she wanted to be Jacque Cousteau, but her first few science-based jobs pointed clearly towards working with people. She worked for several years as a community organizer in Indiana and Ohio. Returning to Michigan in 2005, her reputation followed her for challenging people to see *and be* a better version of themselves, and the phone started ringing. Since then, Ellen has built an internationally recognized company supporting individuals and teams in getting better at everyday important interactions.

Ellen is a credentialed PCC-level Executive Coach from the International Coach Federation (ICF), and certified in multiple assessment tools, including the AcuMax Index®, MRG's Leadership Effectiveness Analysis LEA360® and Leadership Culture® assessments, Genos® International's Emotional Intelligence toolkit, and Equine-Guided Learning practices from Innovative Horizons.

Ellen lives in mid-Michigan with her wife, Dani, at least one and as many as three teenagers at any given time, three cats, and a dog with way too much energy.

WHAT NOW?

Are you a Chronic Assumer? Take the quiz and find out! ChronicAssumer.com

Looking for some examples of how to work with me? Here are a few:

- Enroll in the "CHALLENGING Your Leadership Perspective" group coaching course for an opportunity to focus on areas where assumptions are interfering with your success. It's an 8-week small group coaching class for individual enrollment. Learn more by visiting leadquine.com/LPP
- Choose a one-time Leadership Assessment & Goal Setting Session with me by visiting leadquine.com/LAGS

- Does your team need support?
  Visit leadquine.com/for-teams/ to learn all the ways I work with teams through a team coaching model to support their growth and development.
- Need a speaker? I'm not everyone's cup of tea, but I make a lot of people think, and oftentimes laugh. If you're looking for an interactive speaker to shake things up a little bit, I might be right for you. Let's chat. Find a time by visiting calendly.com/talk2ellen/30

If you want to see all the options for yourself (I totally get that), visit LeadQuine.com to explore everything.

I post articles and videos regularly on LinkedIn that are designed to provide value as you travel your own leadership journey. If that interests you, please find me there @EllenPatnaude

Once a month, I send out "The LeadQuine Lowdown" with quick tips, links to helpful info, and the latest of what's happening with me. Sign up at leadquine.com/newsletter and opt out anytime if you're not getting value.

I'm not going to add to the Podcast space with my own, but I'm fun to interview if you have a Podcast looking for guests.

Reach out to chat about all options and possibilities to Info@LeadQuine.com